PA K

Political Education

Currently a debate is in existence as to whether political education — or indeed political argument of any kind — should be kept out of the classroom. There are those who argue that political education is synonymous with indoctrination and others who suggest that education is by its nature political. For those who agree that there should be a distinct political aspect of the curriculum which instils political knowledge and awareness, there is of course the question of where the emphasis should be placed. How is it possible to achieve any kind of balance? This book analyses the debate about the introduction of courses in political education to secondary, tertiary, and adult education as well as to youth work. It also examines the introduction of an element of political education to specific subjects. It puts forward an argument for political education and discusses what it should consist of and how it should be undertaken.

Robert Brownhill and Patricia Smart are both Lecturers in the Department of Educational Studies at the University of Surrey.

NEW PATTERNS OF LEARNING SERIES
Edited by P.J. Hills, University of Cambridge

POLITICAL EDUCATION

Robert Brownhill
and
Patricia Smart

R

ROUTLEDGE
London and New York

First published 1989
by Routledge
11 New Fetter Lane, London EC4P 4EE
29 West 35th Street, New York, NY 10001

© 1989 R. Brownhill and P. Smart

Printed and bound in Great Britain by
Biddles Ltd, Guildford and King's Lynn

British Library Cataloguing in Publication Data

Brownhill, R.J. (Robert J)
    Political education. — (New patterns of learning
    series)
    1. Great Britain. Educational institutions.
    Political education
    I. Title II. Smart, Patricia III. Series
    320'07'1041

    ISBN 0-415-00593-0

Library of Congress Cataloging in Publication Data

Brownhill, R.J. (Robert J.)
    Political education / Robert Brownhill & Patricia Smart.
        p. cm. — (New patterns of learning series)
    ISBN 0-415-00593-0
    1. Political science — Study and teaching — Great Britain.
    I. Smart, Patricia. II. Title. III. Series.
    JA88.G7B76 1989
    320'.07'041 — dc 19   88-32297
                                                  CIP

CONTENTS

INTRODUCTION

There is a developing interest in political education. At the
September 1984 annual conference of the Politics Association (the professional body of politics teachers in the
United Kingdom), Mr Robert Dunn, M.P., Under-Secretary of
State for Education, made a statement on political
education in schools. He made it clear that he was speaking
for the Department of Education and Science, and stressed
that political education had a valid place in the curriculum,
as political literacy was a prerequisite of adult citizenship.
He argued that it could be taught separately or indirectly
through other subjects and that its content should include
not only information about the machinery of government
and the decision-making process but also political skills. It
should also embody certain values: consideration for the
views of others and respect for free democratic procedures
and the rule of law. However, political education should not
be indoctrination; sensitive issues should be treated in a
balanced and professional manner.

Experience and Participation: Report of the Review
Group on the Youth Service in England had also stressed in
1982 the need for political education amongst young adults.[1]
The Advisory Council for Adult and Continuing Education
(ACACE) published a report in 1985 on Political Education
for Adults.[2] This was followed by a WEA pamphlet, The
WEA and Political Education, January 1985,[3] backed up by a
national seminar held at London University, March 1985, on
Adult Education and Political Education. The speakers
included an HMI and party spokesmen.

A lecturer has been appointed in political education at
the Institute of Education, London University. The Department of Education and Science has commissioned a
Curriculum Review Unit to undertake a survey of political
education in schools and FE colleges, and an investigation of
the training of teachers in that area.

The Curriculum Review Unit has carried out a survey of
initial training courses in political education and has since
set up a group to prepare recommendations for the provision
of courses for political education (see Bedford Papers 16,
1983).[4] The group argues that all teachers should have a
general awareness of the scope of political education, and

should understand the political dimensions of their own subject specialisms and classroom teaching. There are many other recommendations.

There is thus considerable interest in developing political education in secondary, tertiary, and adult education, and in youth work. This has the backing of governmental reports and funding and of HM Inspectorate. A Master's course in political education has been introduced at the London Institute. At Surrey University, a political education option is offered on the M.Sc. in Educational Studies course; political education is included in the Post Graduate Certificate in the Education of Adults course for youth workers; a number of day and weekend schools for teachers in secondary and further education in the area of political education have also been run there.

Nevertheless, it would be true to say that the present government remains ambivalent in its attitude towards political education: recognizing that there should be political education but fearing that it would be misused. Indeed we have noticed in conversations with Conservative politicians that there has been a retreat from the degree of enthusiasm expressed by Mr Dunn. We feel that the government is wrong in reducing their enthusiasm. At this time, when there is wide media cover of political events, it is important that people do not feel that they have no say, that events just pass them by, and that they are mere pawns in a game played by others. A healthy body politic can exist only when people understand the workings of its institutions and are prepared to participate in the working of them and perhaps in their development.

This book opens with an examination of the political education debate and in the next few chapters looks at the relationship between politics, morality, education, and the nature of the political community. We then examine the content of a political curriculum and how it should be taught. In effect, we ask a number of questions - what is the nature of politics, why should there be political education, what would be its content, how should we teach it? - and attempt to provide answers.

Do we as authors agree on all of the arguments? Generally our views do not greatly diverge. Specifically Patricia Smart has been responsible for developing the main lines of argument in the chapters on political argument and indoctrination, and Robert Brownhill for the rest.

While the book should be of particular interest to

teachers and administrators in secondary and further education, adult education, and youth work, it will also be of general interest to students of politics who have an interest in moral, political, and social education.

Chapter one

POLITICAL EDUCATION: THE DEBATE

That education and the political structure of society are closely linked has probably always been recognized. Plato, in his Republic, designed a system of education not only to produce the right outlook and frame of mind in his future leaders but also to sift out those people who should not be leaders. People dominated by their appetites for power, wealth, or glory but also the more stupid, those who could not be 'turned towards the light': Plato hoped to classify them accurately and persuade them to accept their classification. In order to do this, he desired to give them that which they naturally deserved. For example, the menial by nature received menial tasks and so, if they received whatever by nature they deserved, they could not claim that they were being treated unjustly. Plato's system of education was designed to support and maintain his hierarchical community but the political nature of his curriculum for leadership and subordination was hidden. The curriculum was ostensibly designed to turn people towards the light, to lead them to an understanding of reality. The participants in the programme did not know, and had no need to know, its political nature.

It can well be argued that all systems of education have a political nature, that they are designed to initiate children into the traditional ways of going about things. Indeed, we find R.S. Peters including this idea in his definition of education.[1] Education, in this sense, must be conservative and give support to the status quo. At the same time, it leads people to look at the world in a certain way. It gives them the categories of right and wrong and true and false, and tells them how normative claims and truth claims can be classified according to these categories.[2] It provides them with an interpretative framework which will enable

1

them to understand the world, make judgements about it, and cope with innovations.

The development of universal education in nineteenth-century England came about not only because it was thought that ignorance and illiteracy were bad in themselves but also for a number of political reasons. As the century progressed and economic and industrial competition increased, with the growing industrialization of other powers, it became necessary to create a more educated population. For instance, in 1868, Thomas Huxley told the South London Working Men's College that three classes of men favoured education: 'Politicians would educate their masters, manufacturers wanted more efficient hands, the clergy desired to stem the drift towards infidelity.'[3]

However, industrialization had brought with it a much deeper political problem. As the population had moved from the rural areas to the towns, the ties of traditional authority had broken down. There was an urgent need both to adapt to the rapidly changing structure of society and to reassert the authoritarian and hierarchical nature of the community. The French Revolution, which was contemporaneous with the politicians of the earlier part of the century, and the revolutions throughout Europe in 1848 had made many people believe that strikes, riots, and political demonstrations were a prelude to similar happenings in Britain. Kay-Shuttleworth, as early as 1839, had argued that a good secular education would be an antidote to the dangers of Chartism.[4] In a sense, then, the rapidly developing bureaucracy and the introduction of universal education that was controlled and inspected were facets of this adaptation. Education was an instrument of social control. It taught respect for one's betters and the acceptance of authority, and created a population used to discipline.

The elimination of illiteracy and the strengthening of the economic base so that Britain could compete more effectively with industrial rivals was open government policy and therefore could be widely discussed in the development of the curriculum. However, although respect for authority and the necessity for greater discipline were aired in the debate leading up to universal education, they dropped out of the debate when universal education was adopted in England. They constituted the hidden curriculum.

The fact that there is a hidden political curriculum can be seen when society is again in crisis, with high unemployment, unruly youngsters, and the breakdown of communal homogeneity. One of the first criticisms to be levelled is that the educational system is not doing its job: children and young adults are not disciplined, are not used to accepting authority, and do not show respect for their elders. The hidden curriculum is not being followed and democracy is in danger of collapse.

In fact, as has often been pointed out, the traditional, authoritative nature of school education provides little incentive for the vast majority of the population to make decisions for themselves or to participate in decision making. The majority of children need not make any educational decisions, which are made for them. This results in a major part of the population not only being apathetic and leaving decision making to others but also having been conditioned into apathy. The hidden curriculum was designed both to keep discipline and to allow the political establishment to get on with its job of governing without too much interference.

It can be argued that the type of political analysis which we have made of the educational system is normal, radical clap-trap; that a much more important feature of education in the late nineteenth and early twentieth centuries was the development of liberal education, particularly in grammar and public schools and at university. This has led to a much wider knowledge of Britain's cultural heritage and to remarkable developments in the sciences. A feature of liberal education has been its ability to lead pupils into the academic disciplines or modes of experience,[5] where they are taught to love a subject for its intrinsic worth, to reason, to present good arguments and, above all, to love the truth. In this great liberal tradition of education, politics is irrelevant. It is distasteful or even wicked to introduce the activity of politics into the classroom. Politics, like sex, should be kept out of schools. It is an adult activity and children should not be contaminated by it.

Although we agree that the idea of a liberal education is of major importance in the development of the British educational system, we shall argue that the liberal concept of education includes a certain concept of politics. Indeed, some of its exponents do themselves admit that it has within it its own hidden curriculum of political education.

POLITICAL EDUCATION: ARGUMENTS IN FAVOUR

Arguments in favour of political education come from both right and left of the political spectrum. The philosopher and educationalist, Nicolas Haines, opens his book, Person to Person,[6] by asking two questions:

> How many people in our free society find that their education helps much when it comes to making up their minds on major issues outside their field?
> How many educated people seriously believe in their larger political and social role?
>
> (Haines 1967: xi)

He is making the point that growing specialization in higher education has made people less competent and knowledge-able in areas outside their speciality; that their education, rather than widening their horizons, has limited them to such an extent that they have no desire either to participate in or to show an interest in the activity of politics. Yet, he argues, modern society depends very much on a growing, educated middle class. If society is to remain free and not to be controlled by a bureaucracy then an educated professional class must be prepared to take an interest in 'the connection between their own jobs, their personal aims, their principles and the changing, shifting emphasis in politics and reconstruction' (ibid., p. xi).

Haines' argument is not so much that democracy means that everyone should participate in political decision-making but that the major wealth-generating class should at least be prepared to participate. Unfortunately, little attempt is made in the educational system to prepare the new professional classes for such participation. This is a major criticism of the education system. He is arguing that the very group that one would expect to be educated in the running of a free society is not being so educated: 'Free men have to decide, to choose: to elect representatives, support or undermine policies, advocate, persuade, guide, teach, as well as manage, their own affairs as well as they are able' (ibid., p. xii).

The new professional classes are not receiving the sort of education that would enable them to take on the mantle of responsibility which would lead to the protection of freedom. The aim of political education should therefore be to develop the professionals' interest in politics and to point them towards their political responsibilities, while at the same time endeavouring to give them the necessary knowledge and skills to carry out those responsibilities.

Haines' real concern is with a growing bureaucracy and a collectivist movement which he sees as destroying traditional notions of freedom.[7] He is elitist only within the Hayekian liberal/conservative tradition. This recognizes that the defence of political freedom must realistically come from the middle class and points out that collectivist attitudes often downgrade the working class. Collectivist leaders 'over-indulge and pet it with permissive principles and cloying values as if the working class were without moral and intellectual potential - rather as many white people used to think and talk of the Negroes' (Haines 1967: xiv).

Behind Haines' book lay a clear, radical, political intention to oppose collectivism by a programme of political education that would point out how the collectivist society limited people's freedom by taking decisions for them and thereby preventing them from acting responsibly. Haines hoped to educate people in such a way that they would wish to and be able to make their own decisions. The vanguard of the newly politically educated would be the professional classes but the ideal of the future liberal/conservative society would be political education for everyone and a desire on the part of everyone to participate in political matters. The danger that lay behind Haines' proposals and that was part of his nightmare was that the very professional classes (such as social workers, local government officers, teachers - the new professionals), who must be educated into participating in a free society, might themselves see an advantage and self-interest in developing the growing bureaucracy and collective, and therefore provide a weaker line of defence than he hoped. The intention of the book was radical but the book itself was low key, as was its sub-title, 'A work book in principles and values'. In the preface the author stated that it might be useful for groups run by the Workers' Educational Association, for groups of undergraduates in Political and Social Philosophy, and for General or Liberal Studies Courses in Higher Education.

Denis Heater takes up a wider but related theme in a series of books.[8] He stresses that it is the very logic of democracy that citizens should be politically literate, by which he means that adults should be able, in a representative democracy, to make a reasoned choice between candidates and parties at elections, and should perhaps be prepared to take part in some grass-roots activity. If a representative democracy is to work as such, people must be shown how to understand and to use democratic institutions. People cannot be expected to understand, participate in, and make use of democratic institutions, let alone take an interest in them, unless they have been brought up to appreciate them and given some ability to participate in them. They must see why democratic institutions and procedures are so good and why it is worth while having them, and must be able to taste for themselves some of the benefits that can come only from participation. In order to achieve this, not only must children be taught about politics and be given the necessary skills to participate but the institutional structure of their schools must allow them to take part in decision making.

Thus the argument is that the logic of representative government demands political education, because if one desires the end one must also desire the means to that end. Unfortunately, the United Kingdom, although formally a representative democracy, does not have the complete features of an ideal model of such a democracy, simply because not enough people know how it works or participate in its working.

Another assertion is often attached to this sort of argument. The political system of the United Kingdom has a stability and continuity which presumably arises because of its democratic nature. This stability cannot be taken for granted and there is some evidence that there is a growing disillusionment with the system: for instance, the student troubles of the late 1960s; the influence of the extreme left and the extreme right on the major parties; the riots in Bristol, Liverpool, and Birmingham; perhaps also the pressure for devolution in the 1970s.[9] It is suggested, therefore, that it is necessary to teach people the benefits of a democracy so that they will not become disillusioned with it. A more radical suggestion, following the same line of argument, is that the present system of democracy should be developed in such a way as to encourage greater participation and so make it effective. It will thus help to create or preserve a stable society. The idea of continuity can also be maintained by an argument which, in looking at the historical development of British democracy, points out that, in order to maintain the evolutionary development of the system

6

rather than chance revolutionary change, we must progress to the next stage of democracy, which would include greater citizen participation.

In support of these arguments, evidence is produced by Robert Stradling to show the political illiteracy of school-leavers.[10] However, this evidence becomes relevant only if the thrust of the previous arguments is accepted, i.e. that political education is now necessary and is not taking place. A questionnaire was issued to 4,000 15 to 16-year olds between 1975-6. Bernard Crick, Chairman of the Working Party, A Programme for Political Education, writes in the preface to Stradling's study:

> Consider, for example, that almost half of the young people taking part in this survey think that the House of Commons makes all the important political decisions on the running of the country; that 46 per cent cannot name even one pressure group; that one in four fifteen-year-olds associates the policy of nationalisation with the Conservative Party; and that 44 per cent believe that the I.R.A. is a Protestant organisation.
>
> (Stradling 1977: ii)

Stradling concludes his study with the comment that there is something paradoxical about a democracy in which 80 to 90 per cent of its future and present citizens know so little about local and national politics; they not only do not know what is happening but also do not know how they are affected by it or what they can do about it.

The evidence can also be used for a straightforward academic argument in support of improved general education about the nature of politics. The hope of educationalists is that children at 16 years of age will emerge from their schooling with something more than just an ability to read and write and do simple arithmetic, namely some knowledge of literature, history, and geography, for example. We would consider children ill-educated if they did not have a smattering of such knowledge but should we not also consider them ill-educated if they do not have some knowledge of the theory and practice of politics, since politics cannot help but have a major influence on their future lives? They are bound to come into contact with political arguments and to make decisions that have a political element. The very nature of modern life at work and leisure will bring them into contact with political and governmental policy and action.

7

Political education: the debate

There has been a considerable amount of governmental and semi-official support for political education. As mentioned in the Introduction, Mr Robert Dunn, M.P., Under-Secretary of State for Education, made a statement on 'Political Education in Schools' at the 1984 Annual Conference of the Politics Association. He argued that political education had a valid place on the curriculum because political literacy was one of the prerequisites of adult citizenship. He said that in Britain the education system would not be expected to enforce a single political philosophy 'as would be, and is, required in a totalitarian state'. Nevertheless, schools have a responsibility to the society that maintains them and so certain approaches would have to be followed, such as 'respect for the process of democracy itself'.[11]

Regarding the education of the 16 to 19-year old group, further support is given to the introduction of political education. The report, Experience and Participation: Report of the Review Group on the Youth Service in England, states:

> In a democratic society it is inevitable and desirable that there should be a diversity of ideas and opinions. Our political tradition depends on consensus being reached on various issues. While it is accepted that differences cannot always be resolved, an understanding of and respect for the views of others lies at the very heart of a civilised and organised society. This involves a certain level of political literacy. ... Political education then is necessary. ... If they had a better knowledge of the processes by which change can be effected and greater skill and confidence in using them... they would be less likely to resort to more violent methods of expressing their views about society.[12]

Here we find the usual argument about political literacy being necessary, something about its content, and the further argument that people would be less likely to use violence if they understood the process of politics. In all governmental and quasi-official statements, something is said about the nature of politics: that in its practice people should be non-violent, show respect for others, and listen to other people's points of view.

A major reason for the newly found interest in political education evinced by establishment political parties is an increasing fear that there is a growing apathy towards and disillusionment with the British parliamentary system. It is hoped that programmes for political literacy may revive support for the system and head off more radical forms of decision making. Political education in this sense is therefore seen as a way of defending the status quo. However, as has already been pointed out, political education probably provides the base for a further democratization of society, an event that may not be so attractive in some official circles.

Political education, indeed education itself, has trad-itionally been seen by the Labour Movement as a vehicle for change. It has been associated with the idea of education for the underprivileged. An understanding of the political system has been regarded as a necessary step in bringing about the reform of economic and political institutions. This emphasis on the importance of education is based on a belief that knowledge itself is power, that it is useful in bringing about change, and that political knowledge is especially useful. This belief was reflected in the demands of the Chartists but was also a component of that held during the formation of the Workers' Educational Association. That such advocacy for political education comes from the conservative left may not disturb the political establishment but a similar cry coming from the far left may well stir up political ogres and be counter-productive. In any case, it is likely that an emphasis on traditional attempts at political education, as exhibited in WEA and university extra-mural courses on politics, will appeal only to the few who already have such an interest. It deepens or supports their interest rather than creating it. Professor Ridley, following this line of argument, states that 'the social effects of education for citizens are likely to be marginal'.[13] He argues that political education, to be effective, should aim at being practical. It should concentrate on what he calls 'role-oriented political education' which is concerned with such groups as tenants' associations, environmental groups, parents' groups, etc. He argues: 'Many of these are at a disadvantage in dealing with authority, compared to older-established bodies, because their members lack the information base/operating skill which comes naturally to middle class organisers (Ridley 1985: 15). The idea is to concentrate on the practical issues of immediate interest to all groups rather than general, great issues of political debate.

9

Political education: the debate

Ridley, of course, is going along with the idea that knowledge is power and so will lead to the greater democratization of society, but he is arguing that the traditional approach of political education, where great issues are examined, is irrelevant to the groups who most need to take an interest in political education. Political education should be concerned with helping certain underprivileged groups to achieve 'practical benefits ... within a reasonable time span' (Ridley 1985: 9). He therefore puts great emphasis on the activist and participatory function of political education. The concern is not so much to create political literacy or to improve political knowledge (which may, in the long run, further the interests of the Labour Movement) but actively to benefit the underprivileged.

The advocates of political education can be roughly divided into give groups: those who want to preserve the status quo but think that at present, in a changing society, political education is necessary (Haines 1967); those who wish to preserve the status quo but feel that open political education is counter-productive (Oakeshott)[14]; those who believe in a participating democracy but at a restrained level: their ideal is something like Aristotle's polis corrected to the idea that the British system is rather like it but flawed (Porter,[15] Stradling 1977); those who believe in greater activism, aimed at getting the underprivileged to know how to work the system (Ridley 1985); a more radical group who dislike the political set-up and believe that political education could undermine it.

The advocates of political education will quite naturally have different views about the content of political education, the nature of politics, and the nature of society. For instance, liberal educationalists, such as Porter and Stradling, believe that in a participating democracy akin to their own the values of tolerance, respect for others, and rational argument should be emphasized. They believe that politics can exist only when these values are followed. British society is perhaps unjust, with unfair inequalities, but through the process of politics it will gradually improve. On the other hand, a Marxist-Leninist, for instance, would believe that the notion of a participating democracy is a sham, that the education system is designed to preserve the class structure, that political education should be concerned with raising working-class consciousness and exposing the corruption and class character of British society, and that political action is ultimately bound to be violent.

POLITICAL EDUCATION: ARGUMENTS AGAINST

Opposition to the implementation of political education comes from a number of sources and different points of view. It can be argued, for instance, that those supporting a participatory democracy fail to recognize the real nature of British politics and replace it by an ideal too far from reality. British politics is not a sort of enlarged Aristotelian polis where everyone is an equal citizen with a right to have a say and, indeed, a duty to do so. The British people prefer the quiet life and have little or no interest in politics; we can say that their genius lies in their political apathy. The notion of a desire for the quiet life and political apathy go hand in hand and favour the status quo. If one indulges in political education then one must either be deluded about the nature of British politics or have a desire to stir up things in order to make the situation more volatile. One must believe that change is needed and therefore one must be to the left of the political spectrum.

This sort of argument could be a cynical response to arguments in favour of participatory politics or could reflect a different notion about the nature of politics, for instance, Samuel Beer's conception of 'Tory democracy'.[16] Under this conception it is recognized that universal suffrage has occurred but that participation is really confined to little more than a very occasional judgement on election day about the performance of the government (a section of the ruling class). In reality a section of the ruling class, who have the necessary skills and knowledge, attempt to identify the public interest and govern in accordance with it. Indeed it is their function and duty to do so. Under such a concept, which argues that on these grounds of function and duty a political hierarchy can be justified and general participation is not necessary, legitimacy for élite rule is claimed. It is also argued that general participation is not desirable, as the masses do not have the necessary skills and knowledge to rule.

A similar argument has been used from the left of the political spectrum - if we can still call ideas from the Fabians of the thirties and forties left wing. For instance, Sir Julian Huxley, in the thirties, spoke about a new millennium that could be brought about by following scientific principles in the organization of society and industry.[17] This planned society would be led by the experts, the scientists and the scientifically minded, who could

11

conceive how this planning would take place, and the direction that society should take. In other words, these experts had a better insight into the public interest than the masses. This neo-Platonic Fabian elitism paid lip service to participatory democracy but in reality it needed only a low level democracy to legitimate the elite's claim that they were guardians of the public interest. Real political education was not necessary and would even be counter-productive. What was needed was a muted programme of education which would create enough political awareness amongst the general public to allow them to be manipulated, while at the same time making them believe that they were participating in decision making. As Huxley stated, planning should be 'by permission, consent and participation'.

In fact, in both the notion of 'Tory democracy' and Fabian élitism this low level of political education could take place: for instance, recognizing that the country is a representative democracy, and that the governing class or experts are concerned with the public interest and the general welfare of the population. The creation of at least this level of political awareness is even desirable as, paradoxically, it could create political apathy and legitimize the democratic government. It could create John Locke's tacit consent.

A common argument used against political education is aimed at the would-be educators. It asks, 'Who are these educators?', and gives the answer that they are usually the politically active: the trendy lefty and the nasty righty, people who have an axe to grind and hate British democracy. These Trotskyites and members of the National Front desire only to indoctrinate young people in their own 'disgusting' ideologies. Although the fear of indoctrination from the left is more intense than that from the right, care is taken to associate them with the ogres of both persuasions. We can cope with a few right-wing nuts, we meet them in any bar; it is the radical undermining of the established system, the sowing of the seeds of revolution by sinister intellectuals of the left that we must watch.

The writings of Roger Scruton provide an example of this sort of attack on political educators.[18] He and his co-authors argue that these people have a 'political world-view' and consider that every decision, issue, activity, or pursuit stands inside the political arena: that, although this view is now associated with the left, it was originally part and parcel of the view of the National Socialists in Germany.

They argue: 'We can understand the impulse towards indoctrination and the nature of indoctrination itself, only if we see its intrinsic connection with the "politicised" world view' (Scruton et al. 1985: 10).

Everything is regarded in political terms and the question is posed whether it will bring nearer the Marxist concept of social justice or whether it is a barrier against it. Thus, the whole curriculum becomes politicized and is used as a means to bring about the Marxian Utopia.

Clearly, Scruton is politically opposed to Marxist ideology but he also has philosophical objections to their political and philosophical stance, and activity. For instance, Marxist ideology holds that in a capitalist society justice is class justice and will favour the interests of the ruling class. True justice lies in the future and will come about only when a communist society is established. The aim of revolutionary politics therefore lies in its attempt to bring about this future situation, and everything can be used as a means to that end. Thus, the indoctrination of children, indicating the present iniquities of capitalism and the future benefits of a communist society, would be entirely justified.

Traditionally it has been argued that Marx discovered the scientific laws of human development and perceived what future society was going to be like (some Marxists would argue 'could be like'). On the model of nineteenth-century physics, it was argued that the truth was manifest, i.e. we could be certain about some of our beliefs and that these beliefs were objective since they were based on the impersonal laws of human development.

Two major objections have been made to these claims: a practical objection, that society cannot be studied in the same way as a scientist studies his subject matter because society is too complex for a scientific study, and a theoretical objection, that in principle we cannot use the scientific approach to study society. As science is largely concerned with measurement - it uses a quantitative approach - it can give only trivial information about society. A combination of the two arguments can also be used. Society is too complex and cannot be studied by scientific means so, for instance, the attempt to find and apply laws of historical development would rule out many actual events in history and, in any case, historical events are unique and unrepeatable.[19] The conclusions of these types of arguments are that Marx uses the wrong method for his study of society, because scientific laws of historical development cannot be found, and that he fails to understand the nature of history, i.e. he should not be looking for laws of development. More devastatingly, he actually fails to understand the nature of science.[20]

The truth is not manifest.[21] We can never be absolutely certain that we have arrived at the truth, so even the so-called certainties of science are tentative and will remain so forever. All of the laws of science are provisional and may change as further evidence comes to light and hypotheses develop. If this is so then there can be no justification for a Marxist to teach the laws of historical development as certainties or to argue that the true social justice is known and that therefore we are justified in using any means to bring about this objectively perceived end. In any case, we cannot arrive at a concept of social justice through scientific analysis because it is value laden and depends on our commitments and value judgements. As Hayek has pointed out,[22] it is therefore not the function of government to bring about a perceived concept of social justice: a good for one person is not necessarily a good for another.

Sir Karl Popper, in developing this line of attack on Marxism, also challenged its claim that it is scientific. His main objection was that it does not produce its theories in a form that will allow them to be tested. Marxism by its very approach cannot be properly objective and therefore cannot really claim to be scientific.

However, in recent times there has been considerable criticism of the idea that science is an objective pursuit. It is argued that scientific theories can be neither verified nor falsified; the logical positivists and Popper are misguided in their claims that scientific theories can be objectively tested. Taken to its extreme, we get Feyerabend's remark that the choice of one scientific theory over another is a matter of taste, that there is no scientific method as such, and that scientists do not hold their theories on rational grounds.[23] If we accept this type of argument we really have only two alternatives: complete inertia, since there is no point in undertaking scientific research if it is mere prejudice, or a commitment to our belief that the truth can be discovered; scepticism or faith. Neo-Marxists tend to accept this recent subjectivist attack on the objectivity of science and, as they have a ready-made faith with a 'politicized' world view so that everything has political connotations, their commitment must be a political commitment.

This position has the advantage that neo-Marxists need not develop the sophistry and skill in argument of the traditional Marxists, since they know that the so-called objective arguments of their opponents are in reality also a reflection of their opponents' fanatical commitments. Intellectual life is therefore seen as a jihad, a holy war of one set of beliefs against another. In educational terms it means that any attempt to provide an objective approach to curriculum content, such as Hirst's attempt to argue that the forms of knowledge should be included in the curriculum,[24] is misguided. As knowledge is relative and subjective then the necessary content of the curriculum is that which will further Marxist beliefs and goals.

Of course if one is to be entirely successful in an attack on neo-Marxists, one must point out not only that their position leads to relativism and a reliance on commitments but also that their position is incoherent, and that one can be objective and justify the inclusion of certain subjects in the curriculum and not others. This is a task that is not yet satisfactorily accomplished. An argument connected with the Scrutonian view, and opposed to the 'politicized' world view, is that politics is at best peripheral to the real needs of young people. It is, in reality, just another subject that some advocates claim should be included in the curriculum. It should therefore be treated as such and financed accordingly. There may be an argument for teaching political history and civics but there is something rather strange about teaching young people to be politically active. Political activity is for an older age group; a proper understanding of politics can come only with age and experience. If we wish to apply utilitarian concerns to education then we should concentrate on giving young people work training, and our concern should not be politically oriented.

A powerful argument against political education, which takes up this point that it is rather odd to teach young people political skills, is developed in the writings of Michael Oakeshott and Michael Polanyi.[25] We shall briefly examine here their arguments as related to political education but will return to them in a wider context in Chapter 3. Oakeshott, in discussing the nature of education, points out that it is a very long process whereby pupils have to accept much on authority until they have properly learned the language of a subject.[26] Indeed it is not until the pupils have arrived at university that they will begin to have the ability to criticize and contribute anything at all to a subject. They have to be led into a discipline by a teacher, shown its nuances, its techniques, and its art before they can even begin to move towards any degree of independence. Clearly very few pupils can be expected either to achieve this degree of learning or to learn properly the language of a discipline. The idea that pupils can or even should learn to be critical at an early age is therefore nonsense. They have to take a good deal on trust and cannot be expected to develop meaningful criticism until they thoroughly understand the nature and language of a discipline.

The same argument applies to politics. Politics is an art which we can only gradually learn through experience and by watching and listening to others. Oakeshott, in his theory of learning, makes a distinction between instructing a pupil with chunks of information and imparting the skill and know-how that go with it. The imparting of skill and know-how is not consciously passed on by the teacher but is picked up by the pupil through watching, listening, and eventually by practising. All information, if it is going to be eventually used, must be associated with the necessary skills and understanding that go with it. Thus the ability to understand and practise politics can be gained only by experience within a political set-up, by an apprenticeship. In the same way that one cannot learn to be a good cook by merely reading a cookbook, one cannot learn to be a ruler by reading Machiavelli's The Prince.

Associated with Oakeshott's theory of learning is another theory about the nature of knowledge. When an explicit statement is made, the statement will have little meaning in itself but can be understood only by looking at its context. It will be surrounded by a range of other beliefs and references to which the listener must be attuned if he/she is to understand the true meaning of the explicit statement. Likewise, if the speaker expresses or even holds a piece of information or knowledge that he/she perceives clearly and distinctly, then this piece of information or knowledge will also be surrounded by subsidiary beliefs and opinions which the speaker does not express and may not even fully understand or recognize.

Michael Polanyi, in developing a similar theory of learning to Oakeshott, makes a distinction between tacit knowledge and explicit knowledge. Explicit knowledge can be understood only within a framework of tacit knowledge but the extent of tacit knowledge can never be completely revealed, as one piece of knowledge will always rely on subsidiary beliefs and opinions. We can never reveal or express all of our beliefs. For Polanyi this concept of tacit and explicit knowledge is applied equally in the physical and intellectual fields and is the reason why we cannot teach certain skills. The skills have to be imparted by the teacher and picked up by the pupil. As Polanyi states, 'We know more than we can say'; thus, for instance, in teaching someone to play golf, the correct stance can be shown, the swing can be corrected, the position of the head may be altered but we cannot teach someone to be a good golfer, as something else is missing. This can be obtained only by continuous practice and by watching and copying a master. The same argument is used in the case of a historian or scientist. The ability to be a good scientist or historian has to be picked up by the pupil working with a master within a community that is concerned with science and history. The pupil has to absorb the traditions of the community and the style of the master before he/she can hope to gain independence and to make original contributions. In order to be good at anything we need continuously to widen our experience, be determined to learn, and to follow the expert in the hope that we may catch on to some of that person's special skills and capacities to judge the right time, the right place, and the right situation to take the appropriate action.[27]

Expertise in politics, as in everything else, can be gained only by the person of experience who has developed the art of political judgement. The argument also says something about the nature of political knowledge. Political values and principles are far from being the whole of political knowledge, as they are merely the abridgements of a particular political tradition. They are drawn out of a surrounding area of tacit beliefs and practices, which are really necessary if the principles and values are going to be properly applied and used. For instance, Edmund Burke, in his Reflections on the Revolution in France, pointed out how the French revolutionaries had withdrawn certain principles and values from English practice and had attempted to apply them in France without having the art and tradition that would enable them to do so.

In broader terms, the argument is that the advocates of political education in schools and youth programmes misunderstand the nature not only of the learning process but also of politics. The attempt at direct political education is inappropriate. At best it will inculcate only poorly understood political principles and values and also a critical attitude without an understanding of what is being criticized.[28] It is bound to entail the indoctrination of pupils with an ideology, i.e. a package of ill-conceived principles and values cut off from other beliefs and practices that give them meaning.

In the writings of Polanyi, the argument is also associated with an argument for liberal education. He argues that the search for truth within the academic disciplines necessarily entails open public discussion, with a respect for rational argument and other people's points of view. Liberal education is concerned with preparing pupils for participation in these disciplines and with giving them an insight into their cultural heritage. In other words, the values which are inherent in traditional British education, and within the different academic disciplines, are also those which are necessary for a free society. He states:

> The ideal of a free society is in the first place to be a good society: a body of men who respect the truth, desire justice and love their fellows. It is only because these aspirations coincide with the claims of our own conscience that the institutions which secure their pursuit are recognized by us as the safeguards of our freedom.[29]

The constitution of a free society and its practices are a reflection of the shared values of the community. The function of the state in such a community is to provide the conditions necessary for the development of these values. As the free society already exists, its tasks are to preserve the present structure of liberal education and to nurture the development of the different intellectual disciplines controlled by their own authority. There is no need for direct indoctrination in the values of a free society because pupils are already being given the values in the normal process of education.

The argument has a number of special features. Intellectual communities, such as the scientific, are controlled by the shared authority of their members and are concerned with obtaining the truth in their different disciplines and revealing it to others. In order to achieve this aim, the members of a community must themselves have a commitment to the truth and recognize that they all have such a commitment. In other words, they are bound together by mutual obligations. It also means that they are obliged to produce and present their discoveries and ideas in a way which will allow them to be publicly discussed and assessed. Each member must be allowed a considerable amount of freedom to undertake personal research, as it is only by individual initiative that new ideas will develop and progress take place. Nevertheless, it is the community as a whole that decides whether or not a particular idea will be accepted as part of the knowledge of that community. However, the individual member, whose idea may have been rejected, can still go on developing related ideas in its support and collecting further evidence in the hope that the community may eventually be persuaded to accept the idea as part of their knowledge.

The intellectual communities are thus authoritative and bound together by traditional values but are also liberal in the sense that they allow individuals to pursue their own research in their own way. The communities are similar in that they develop the systematic ideas of their own disciplines and pursue the truth. The only difference lies in the methods that they use to pursue and assess their truth claims.

Polanyi provides a sketch of how a political community will work in the same way; its traditional values, although not a body of systematic values as in the case of the intellectual communities, will at least be coherent and will allow the community to control and keep a check on innovations. The values inherent in the intellectual communities, with their pursuit of the truth, are the very same values which are needed for a free society. The normal process of liberal education therefore creates the required values for a free society.[30]

The argument is elitist in the sense that only those of superior intellect will get the full value of a liberal education and be able to participate fully in an academic discipline. A similar argument can be used in the case of a political community. However, every person who can produce strong and persuasive arguments will be listened to and, as a member of the community, will have a right to be listened to: respect for others, as intellects, is a characteristic of Polanyi's intellectual communities and of the liberal society.

Polanyi's argument for a free society is in essence very similar to that set out by John Stuart Mill in On Liberty.

Mill's political community, like Polanyi's, is based on an academic community in which participants are concerned with searching for a political truth. The truth is not manifest and therefore all opinions must be allowed so that their rationality can be judged.[31]

This argument, which rejects political education on the grounds that it is not necessary and, if directly attempted, would be a form of political indoctrination, meets a number of difficulties. The argument, as developed by Polanyi, assumes that the political community is like an academic community and is concerned with searching for the truth. It can well be argued that politics is not concerned with achieving a political truth but with making reasonable decisions, often on the basis of inadequate information. Indeed, it is ideological politics that assumes that a political truth is attainable or even that we can approximate to it.[32] Politics, as Oakeshott points out, is not aiming at any particular end; it is far more like a conversation, and the political art is to keep the conversation going.

It does seem to be the case that a liberal education favours certain values which are reflected in a free society, such as open discussion, rational argument, and respect for other people's points of view. However, the full benefits of a liberal education are available only to the few who make full use of it and perhaps enter the academic life. The vast majority of the population do not receive these benefits and probably do not understand the reasons for, or the nature of, the values associated with it. Because one has been taught the value of free and open discussion in the intellectual life it does not follow that one transfers this to the political life. There is a tendency to pigeon-hole concepts and keep them separate from other items of knowledge. In any case, politics is not immediately recognizable as akin to academic life, since it is also concerned with moving people in a desired direction. It is by no means clear to a protagonist that his/her argument will be strengthened by presenting or even listening to an alternative put in its strongest form. The skills of an academic are not immediately recognizable as the necessary skills of a politician.

It is also the case that liberal education is falling into disrepute, not only with the left, claiming that it is elitist and anti-egalitarian, but with the right, claiming that education should be far more vocational. It is therefore likely that traditional liberal education will cease to be the norm in our educational system.

The strength (or plausibility) of the Polanyian idea of a free society reflecting the values inherent in the intellectual communities lies in his claim that there is a coherent political tradition in Britain and that the normal educational system continually reaffirms this tradition. If there ever was a coherent political tradition, the developing multi-cultural nature of modern society must threaten it. Indeed, this is precisely the danger that numerous politicians and political commentators have recognized.

If the concept of a coherent political tradition is rejected then it is difficult to see how it can justifiably be used as an instrument of control, which maintains stability and continuity in the political community, and be said to reflect the characteristic values of the academic communities. In such a case we should surely argue that, since future citizens will not relate the intellectual life to politics, if we think certain values and our concept of politics are important then we should be prepared to teach them directly.

In fact, the opposite conclusion has sometimes been reached. Britain has become a multi-cultural society without a coherent political tradition. It is therefore dangerous to indulge in political education, as differing and conflicting elements in the tradition will vie with each other to be taught. The argument is also associated with that of relativism; if there is no truth or falsity, and only a commitment to beliefs, then any facet of the tradition can be taught.

CONCLUSION

It is clear that the people who combine an argument for liberal education with an argument against political education are taking up a political stance. They believe that the inculcation of the values inherent in liberal education will be instrumental in creating the values of a free political community. We argue, however, that the educational system does not teach, through the normal educational process, the values of a free society or the nature of a political community. The vast majority of the population know very little about them. This being the case, if we are committed to values such as respect for others, social justice, the open society, etc., we must be prepared to tell our pupils about them and to explain why they too should value them.

The situation is becoming urgent. As has been pointed out, in a multi-cultural society, where relativism has become the dominant moral doctrine, it is essential to put over powerfully the argument for a free society and a political society. The task, which is beyond the scope of this book, is to show that a political society is the best society. In so doing, the following must be demonstrated.

1   A political society is better in the moral sense if not in the material sense.

2   It is meaningful to state that the morality of one organizational structure is better than another.

3   Although it may be the case that we can have no certainty in morals, we can have good reasons to prefer one position to another.

4   Although without a commitment to a particular moral stance we are unlikely to have either the will to propound it or the incentive to take action in accordance with it, commitment by itself is not enough.

5   There must be a degree of objectivity in our morality.

6   We must be prepared to make universal claims for certain moral standards and give good reasons for our beliefs.

7   Although politics is wider than morality, since it is also concerned with such things as organization, economics, welfare, and justice, it must have a strong element of morality within it.

8   Essentially a political community is also a moral community.

Chapter two

THE MORAL BASE OF POLITICS AND POLITICAL EDUCATION

As one of the purposes of education is to prepare children for adult life, much of its content will be determed by our ideas about what we believe to be desirable characteristics in the adult human being. In other words, a large proportion of education will be determined by our beliefs about the nature of our own society and the human beings within it. However, it can be seen that there is already scope for disagreement amongst potential educators, as they may have different views about the nature of society and its inhabitants. They may believe that the society in which we live is corrupt and that the way to change it is to educate children for a different sort of society. They may believe that the society in which we live is corrupt but that it cannot be changed and therefore education must be concerned with teaching children to make the best of a bad job. They may believe that society is fairly good and that therefore education should be concerned with emphasizing its desirable qualities and criticizing its undesirable qualities. They may even believe that the type of society in which we live should be entirely rejected and therefore should be criticized and destroyed and that no alternative should be proposed. There are many different views about the nature of society and therefore of the task of the educator. The examination of these alternatives is inevitably part of the task of the educator who is prepared to look at education as a whole.

In a wide sense we can say that this sort of educator is concerned with the philosophy of education, which will reflect his/her values and the notion of how people ought to be. However, in considering how people ought to be, the educator will also be considering them in their relation to each other, in their ethical, social, and political

23

relationships. It is true, of course, that an educator must be concerned with other things, such as when and how to educate, and economic and physical resources. However, when overviewing education, the educator will be concerned not only with the empirically given but also with ideas about how people ought to live and how they should live together.

The philosopher of education will therefore be concerned with setting out general educational aims and with attempts to justify them by reference to general ethical and social values. Once certain aims or goals have become acceptable, the educator will need to consider the things that must be done in order to achieve the ends, and which stage in the educational process we expect our children to have reached at different times in their lives.

We have given the task of considering the aims and goals of education to the philosopher of education, with the further proviso that he/she be concerned with justifying any proposals by reference to general ethical and social values. In that sense the philosopher of education must be concerned with political philosophy, with looking at ideas about the nature of the good life, and with concepts of the good society. Education and politics, as Plato saw long ago, are inevitably linked together.

These views of the tasks of the philosopher of education, and of the political philosopher, have in recent years come in for much criticism. The criticism has arisen from a desire to rule out value judgements and prescriptions from the field of science, and to act as educators and political experts as scientists. It coincides with the belief that value judgements, by their very nature, must be relative, subjective and not justifiable. The argument is that the real task of the philosopher is to engage in second-order activities; for instance, to recognize the experts, the educationalists, and the political scientists, and do no more than examine their concepts and presuppositions. Indeed, conceptual analysis and the examination of presuppositions is the whole task of the modern philosopher.

A number of objections can be made to this argument. It is not at all certain that science is, or can be, free of value judgements. Paul Feyerabend, for instance, argues that scientific judgement is a matter of taste and akin to aesthetic judgement.[1] It is also questionable whether there can be experts in education in the way in which there may be experts in science. It may be possible to talk of the autonomy of science, where science is a discipline in its own right, but it is more difficult to argue in the same way about education. The aims of science are generally accepted by scientists and can be summarized as an attempt to examine nature under the category of quantity: the explanation, prediction and manipulation of nature by the use of general and quantifiable theories. However, the aims of education are not at all clear and there are numerous disputes about what they should be. There is no general consensus about what education is and quite clearly there are different ideas about the content of education in different societies. There are bound to be disputes about the aims of education because the basis of the disputes lies in people's desires and intentions. Yet surely the fact that people argue about educational aims and have different viewpoints cannot be used as grounds to argue that it is not the task of the educator to examine these aims. Value judgements cannot be divorced from education in the way that they can be, doubtfully, divorced from science.

If it is not the task of the educator to propose and justify educational aims then whose task would it be? Is it the job of the politician, the economist, the political philosopher, or scientist? It does not really matter because, in formulating the aims for education, that person must be acting as a high-level educator and therefore must justify proposals by reference to values inherent in society. Thus the philosopher of education can still ask questions about the nature of those values, the criteria being used in their application, and the basis for their acceptance.

There still remains, of course, the ultimate objection that value judgements are basically prejudices which express our feelings and tastes and therefore have no objective validity. It would therefore follow that high-level educational aims provide a framework of prejudices within which we indoctrinate our children, and that all educational proposals are subjective and relative and so one proposal can have no more justification than any other. Such an argument, if accepted, completely destroys the basis of education unless we are prepared to argue that education is designed to show us the futility of our lives and to give us an awareness of its meaninglessness. Of course, such an argument is internally incoherent; if we cannot be objective, then we have no reason to accept the validity of the argument which points to our failure to rise above our own subjectivity. We will return to the question of objectivity later.

25

Politics, like education, is also value laden and politics at a high level is concerned with considering the type of society that we wish to have and the justifications for such a society, and with an examination of possible ways of bringing about such a society. The overview of politics is the task of the political philosopher. As with education, there can be many views about both the society that we should be attempting to achieve and how we should achieve our aims. Traditionally, political philosophy has examined certain problems involving the nature of the good society, political obligation, and social justice. It is at this point that the traditional approach has been criticized, by denying that it is legitimate to move from analysis to prescription. This is part and parcel of the argument that philosophy is a second-order activity and that its proper pursuit is to analyse the concepts of political theory. Clearly, there is a suppressed normative content in the pursuit, and a similar question arises to that made above about the task of education. If it is not the task of the political philosopher to formulate ideas about the good society, social justice, etc., then whose task it it? Surely it is not the political scientist as scientist but perhaps it is the man in the street?

Much of present practice in political philosophy involves what we can call a concept-by-concept approach. For instance, the concept of equality is examined; by analysis it is shown that different approaches can be rejected and that a particular approach is the most sound. The suggestion is not that a particular understanding of, say, equality is proposed but that all right-thinking people, who have thoroughly understood the analysis, will see that the conclusion about the proper meaning of equality is correct and that therefore they should use the term in the same way. A prescription is not being made but people are being led to see the correct meaning of the term by conceptual analysis. Of course, the new method is really an old method protected by a scientific-like cloak to guard it against accusations of prescriptiveness. It does not seem all that different from Plato's persuasive definition of justice in the Republic, leading us to an acceptance of the meaning of justice as equals to be treated equally and unequals unequally.

Our comparison of the concept-by-concept approach to Plato's definition of justice highlights a problem with the approach. If the approach is to be at all successful then the conclusion of each analysis should fit together with that of other political concepts. A piecemeal approach to political concepts is unsatisfactory unless it is part of a general approach to create coherence in political philosophy. It needs to be part of a systematic approach to political philosophy. A major concern of philosophy is to set out clearly the meaning of our concepts (clarity), to make sure our concepts do not contradict each other (consistency), and to see that concepts generally hang together (coherence).[2] The thrust of political philosophy, as surely in all other intellectual pursuits, must be systematically to create order out of chaos.

The concept of wholeness is important and is why it is not possible to separate politics from education. Politics is concerned with all aspects of our lives: what we do, how we live our lives, and how we live together. Its major interest is in the sphere of values, their influence, their basis, and their meaning. It is concerned with the right relationship between values and values, and person and person, so that ultimately its major concern must be the just society: how it ought to be organized, and how it can be expressed through its institutional structure.

How can we find out what is the right relationship, what is the just society, and how the good society ought to be organized? Do we not need some methodological approach, some way of assessing alternative claims? Should not a major concern of political education be to give people the tools to assess the strength of competing claims? Of course, in a way, the study of the classical political philosophers does give us a methodological approach to politics.

For instance, Thomas Hobbes, in the <u>Leviathan</u>, uses a particular sort of methodological approach. He attempts to understand politics by looking at man in the state of nature, and then decides on his characteristics. He then deduces from this analysis what man would need to do if he were going to have any sort of social existence. The method is an attempt at a scientific approach. We look at what man is and not what he ought to be. In so doing we should look at his actual desires, and then ask ourselves what sort of society would be needed to satisfy at least his basic desire for self-preservation. The nature of man necessitates a certain type of society, i.e. we can escape from the state of war, which Hobbes assumes exists in nature, only by creating an all-powerful sovereign. Hobbes' point is not that we ought to create a situation of absolute sovereignty but that of necessity we are bound to, if we desire to create a situation of security, which is the condition necessary for the pursuit of all other values. His method is therefore to examine man in the state of nature and then to deduce from that the form of society needed to meet man's major desire, that for security. The assumptions behind particular methodological approaches are also important. In Hobbes' writings it is the individual who is important. Society is an artificial creation designed by individuals in order to lift themselves out of a state of fear. If this is achieved it then provides the framework for the pursuit of felicity.

John Locke also focuses on the individual in the state of nature but finds him/her altruistic as a rule. Society is needed to protect the individual rights of people. There is no need for an all-powerful sovereign, since people are good on the whole. Indeed, it is best to guard against giving state officials too much power and to tolerate our rulers rather than revere them. Rulers are placed in a position of trust, which can be withdrawn if the rulers go beyond the terms of the trust. Like Hobbes, Locke, by his analysis of man in the state of nature, deduces the type of society that will be needed in order to satisfy man's real desires.

Aristotle, on the other hand, considers man not so much as an individual but as a social animal, who has social virtues. Law/convention and the state arise out of man's nature, and the state also has an educational component in that it has the function of guiding man towards the good society. The ideal state is a natural growth and arises when the growth is not distorted. It is a natural family writ large. It is not therefore an artificial creation but a natural development. In such a state the idea of rights and obligations set against each other is somewhat misplaced, as relationships are much more like those that exist in a family. Aristotle's method is to look at society in its growth, and as a natural phenomenon, whilst recognizing that distortions and anomalies are possible; indeed his experimental methodology of collecting examples of constitutions would have indicated this to him.

There are other methodologies available. For instance, we could look at the characteristics that we think an ideal society should have and then design a Utopia in accordance with those characteristics (Plato's approach). We could ask ourselves what sort of society we would have if we started to create a society from scratch. In doing this we could assume that everyone had equal power or that all lay behind a veil of ignorance, and that no one desired to be treated in a worse way than anyone else (Games theory approach, e.g. that of J. Rawls[3] and probably also that of Hobbes). We could also ask ourselves how a state would be if it were created by a person who had no interest in the outcome (the impartial observer).

A politically educated person needs not only to understand the use and purpose of these different methodological approaches but also to develop the ability to assess the outcome of each different approach. He/she must have on command the tools of the philosopher which will permit an assessment of the logic of the arguments presented (their internal consistency) and of how they hang together (their coherence).

We also need to ask questions such as why did Hobbes develop the methodology he used and was he justified in doing so? Was John Stuart Mill correct in assuming both that a mature, rational adult is concerned with searching for the truth, and that one of the tasks of politics is to get as close to the truth as possible?[4] In such a way we would not only be asking questions about the internal strength of a systematic political theory but also assessing it from the outside by looking at its strengths and weaknesses.

Our argument has come a long way. We have argued that the purpose of education is to prepare children for adult life. The content of education will be partially determined by the ideas that we have about the characteristics desirable in adult life, by our beliefs about our own society and the people within it. However, in order to make adequate decisions, we must consider and assess alternatives developed in our society and perhaps in other societies. As educators we shall be concerned with developing the goals and aims of education and, because of that, we shall be concerned with different values and their justification. We have suggested that, of necessity, we will be undertaking one of the tasks of the philosopher of education, namely to reflect, from an educational view-point, on how people ought to be as individuals and in their relationships with each other. More specifically, we need to look at, and assess, the impact and influence on the curriculum of the values that we hold about our concept of a person and his/her relationships with others. However, in reflecting on how human beings ought to be as individuals and on how they should live together, we would be considering humanity in its ethical and political mode of behaviour. If an ultimate overview is to be achieved, we need to become moral and political philosophers. As such, we would need to develop a systematic understanding of the values inherent in society, an understanding of the different methodologies available, and the ability to assess the strengths and weaknesses of different alternatives from both internal and external points of view. We would require, ideally, an ability to recognize the best alternative or, more realistically, an ability to recognize a flawed alternative. The ultimate educator is the philosopher.

This is far from being a mere theoretical discussion because, in arguing that the ultimate educator must be the philosopher, we are arguing that education's major concerns must be with ethical and social values. Yet education is concerned not only with the inculcation of values but also the development of the abilities to understand and assess values and to act in accordance with the appropriate values. The pupils themselves need to develop the abilities; that is the point of education.

This gives us a clue as to what sort of society we require. We need to have a society that will allow us to use the tools necessary to assess different moral and political values. We need, therefore, a political system that allows, indeed encourages, citizens to criticize; a society that will ask for, listen to, and challenge justifications. A political system that allows only some people to have the ultimate tools of politics, the tools of the philosopher, is incoherent. Politics is ultimately concerned with establishing the good society. In establishing a way of life that people value and desire, we need to provide the tools and methodology for its achievement. The methodology of politics must be part of the art of politics. If it is not included in a system of politics then that system can be only a distortion. Aristotle argued that it is in the nature of man to live in a polis. His ideal polis was where people were equal as citizens but, as he pointed out, there could be many different sorts of states, many deviations from nature. Our argument is akin to this. If politics is concerned with providing the conditions for the good life (or, pessimistically, to avoid the bad life), it needs to allow for the tools of its own pursuit. If it is concerned with the good of the whole, it should take account of the values held by each part, and, if it is concerned with the good of the individuals, it should also take account of what they value. The methodology of politics is part and parcel of the pursuit of politics, and the pursuit of politics is made possible because some people have the necessary skills and abilities to participate in the pursuit. The logic of a political society entails that all citizens have the right to participate in such a society and, from the educational point of view, that all citizens be given the opportunity to understand and develop the abilities to influence such a society. The notion of political education for everyone is really contained within the concept of politics itself.

ON VALUING A POLITICAL SYSTEM

We have argued that the educator should be concerned with the goals and aims of education and with their justification by reference to ethical and social values inherent in society. This leads to a number of questions about the relationship of values to political goals and political organizations. For instance, why should we value certain political goals or value different types of political organizations? What is, or would be, the consequence of the fact that we do or do not value certain goals or organizations? What do we mean by stating that we value something? We value certain political goals because we believe that, if achieved, they will lead to the fulfilment of our desire; we value particular types of organization, or even a whole political system, because they will or are more likely to lead to the achievement of our goals.

The questions and answers can be put in a more traditional form which brings out the normative aspects of political relationships. Traditionally the question would be whether or not we had a political obligation or duty to obey a particular sovereign authority. If we had an obligation, what was the basis for it? Or, to put the questions in a wider context, is politics really an ethical pursuit and does it therefore require people to understand, discuss, and put into effect moral imperatives, or is it the pursuit of power and therefore concerned with the exercise of force?

We recognize that force must be a feature of a sovereign state because sovereign states are closed associations in the sense that generally they are unable to throw out dissenters. They are stuck with the members whom they have. Unlike associations such as clubs or parties or trade unions, they cannot just deny membership to people who flout and reject the rules. They must therefore

31

ultimately have coercive power at their command to uphold the rules and to protect them from obstructions and infractions.

However, we believe that the main feature of political communities is the normative element in relationships. In order to illustrate this, we shall examine the concept of political duty or obligation and bring out (a) the notion of politics as force and power, (b) the notion of politics as being value laden, with the ultimate aim of providing the conditions necessary for our form of life (the way we choose to live).

A.P. d'Entrèves argues that there are really only two models of political obligation: Benthamite and Rousseaunian.[5]

The model based on the writings of Jeremy Bentham[6] includes two basic ideas: first, that you have an obligation if you are subject to either force or the threat of force and, second, that the type of obligation created is dependent on the source of the force or the threat of force. Thus, if the force or threat of force comes from a religious source it is a religious obligation but if it comes from a political source it is a political obligation. The argument is simply that, if force is used against us or if we are threatened, we will obey. The word 'obliged' is being used in a very weak sense and gives us little choice. We will obey or we will be hurt. Of course, we could refuse but we would be very stupid to do so. It is almost like saying, 'If I hold this piece of chalk in my hand above the desk and open my hand, the chalk is <u>obliged</u> to fall on to the desk. It <u>will</u> fall on to the desk.'

The Rousseaunian model, based on the writings of J.J. Rousseau, uses the word 'obliged' in a stronger, more conventional sense. Rousseau states:

> To yield to force is an act of necessity, not of will - at the most an act of prudence. In what way can it be a duty? Let us admit that force does not create right, and that we are obliged to obey only legitimate powers.[7]

Rousseau is clearly using the word 'obliged' in a normative sense, meaning that we value the political power because it is legitimate and, because we value it, we have a duty to obey, protect, and submit ourselves to it. The fact that a political superior has sufficient power at its command to force us to do certain things is not grounds to argue that we have a duty to obey it. We may obey it for prudential reasons but we do not have a duty to obey it. When we use the word 'obligation' in the way in which Rousseau uses it, we are indicating that the performance or non-performance of certain acts is either desirable or non-desirable independently of whether force or the threat of force is being used to push us in one direction or the other.

The Benthamite argument does seem to be internally inconsistent and, if developed properly, could be fitted into the Rousseaunian model of obligation. Jeremy Bentham argues that we are motivated by a desire to maximize pleasure and minimize pain. He states:

> Nature has placed mankind under the government of two sovereign masters, pain and pleasure. It is for them alone to point out what we ought to do, as well as to determine what we shall do. On the one hand the standard of right and wrong, on the other the chain of causes and effects, are fastened to their throne.[8]

Of course, we could argue that this is not morality at all because, under the doctrine of psychological hedonism, individuals will automatically try to maximize pleasure and minimize pain. They will have no choice. We therefore cannot argue that they ought to maximize pleasure but simply that they will. Bentham's analysis of political obligation seems to reflect this confusion. However, if we admit that some choice is possible, we still would not arrive at the concept of political obligation that Bentham gives us. What is happening is that our political superior simply recognizes that we have a duty to ourselves to avoid pain, and then triggers off this duty by the threat of force. The political superior gains obedience but the only duty that arises is the duty to oneself to avoid pain and not to our political superior.

If developed in this way, Bentham's argument would be using the words 'obligation' and 'duty' in the same way as Rousseau, i.e. oneself is of value and therefore should be protected. It would therefore appear that, if we use the term 'political obligation', we mean that the political set-up is of value to us and so we have a duty to protect, obey, and submit ourselves to it.

Rousseau argues that we are obliged to obey only legitimate rulers, by whom he means rulers who have been authorized to express the General Will of the community. We accept that we have a duty to obey legitimate rulers, and by 'legitimate' we mean rulers who have been correctly authorized and accepted by the community, but we believe that legitimacy creates a legal obligation rather than a political obligation. If we have a political obligation we will also have a legal obligation but to have a legal obligation does not mean that we will also have a political obligation.

All political communities need to have a decision procedure, a sovereign authority, and that authority will be concerned with establishing the right rules for governing its own particular society. Its legitimacy lies in the procedure being considered the proper procedure for establishing the rules. Its legitimacy lies in its acceptability.

To be a citizen means belonging to a certain city and living and acting according to the rules. To violate these rules, at least in theory, means to threaten the city. We recognize that rules are necessary to maintain security and to achieve communal goals, and therefore accept the authority of a political power to make the rules. Professor Ross writes about a general attitude towards the law for a state to exist:

> The attitude is as a general rule of a formal character; it is directed towards the institutions with recognition of their validity as such, irrespective of whether the demands in which they manifest themselves can be approved as "morally right" or "just".[9]

This is really a legal obligation, whereas a political obligation is both wider and more personal. The political set-up may not be attractive enough to create a political obligation.

A political obligation exists within a political context: we need to know to whom before we know why we have a political obligation. It consists of an allegiance to a system[10] rather than an acceptance of each rule which the system contains. If we had an obligation we would perhaps value its method of going about things, its institutional structure, or perhaps its methods of settling disputes. We would value the system and not necessarily particular items in it or particular laws. We value a political system because it enables other things to exist that we value. Its value is derived from its ability to provide the conditions necessary for our form of life. That is, it allows us on the whole to value the things that we want to value, and provides conditions to increase the likelihood of the existence of the things that we value.

We have accepted that to say that we have an obligation to something means that we value it and that therefore it should be obeyed, protected, or submitted to, and so a political obligation arises when we begin to value the political system. It can be seen to have arisen when, in spite of the fact that the specific action it undertakes is against an important item in our value systems, we still feel a duty to obey it. This means that we value the system itself rather than the individual items that it enacts, and we value it mostly because it provides the conditions necessary for our form of life. The obligation can be seen to have arisen when we begin to give the system the benefit of the doubt when it seems to be opposed to some of our values in a specific action. This means that the political system, as far as we are concerned, has begun to transcend the items within its own structure and has become for us an entity in itself which we value.[11]

The analysis tells us also when a political obligation will lapse. If laws are being constantly passed which we find repugnant and which are opposed to our own values then this can develop until we realize that the state is no longer providing the conditions necessary for the survival of our values. Its value in the first place was derived from its extrinsic worth in allowing the things that we value. If it no longer has this extrinsic worth, it is no longer of value to us. We therefore no longer have a duty to submit ourselves to it or a political obligation to obey it.

We have expressed this notion of the political system failing to 'coincide with the claims of our own conscience'[12] as a failure to provide the conditions necessary for our form of life. More generally we can say that if a political system allows the continued existence of our form of life or, more specifically, if it furthers it, then we have an obligation towards it since it values the things that we value. If it does either of these things then it is difficult to see how a political obligation can exist.

At this point it is necessary to explain our use of the term 'form of life'.[13] We mean a set of value systems each of which belongs to a different point of view, for instance, moral, religious, aesthetic. If it is possible to know a person's form of life, it should be possible to tell which system of values will be relevant in a particular case and which system will take precedence in a conflict. In order to illustrate this and the interplay of different value systems, consider the case of a member of an activist minority group organization who blows up a bridge, and the judge who conducts the subsequent trial.

Four value systems seem important here for the member of the activist organization:

1   The legal system: how far, for instance, does the activist value the legal system? Presumably he/she recognizes that an illegal act challenges the structure of society.
2   Political values: are political values of such importance that they can lead the activist to reject his/her legal obligation to obey the law?
3   Moral values: what disvalue does the activist place on blowing up other people's property?
4   Prudential values: the threat of arrest and punishment.

In the case of the judge we are able to catch a glimpse of the communal form of life. Three value systems seem important:

1   The value of the integrity of the legal system: that for the continued existence of the legal system, laws should be applied, obeyed and enforced.
2   The value of the communal moral value system: according to Lord Devlin, a judge must uphold public morality.[14]
3   The community's political value system, and especially the value of compromise: J.A.C. Griffith points out that in practice judges are not isolated from reality, as legal theory tells us they should be, but do take note of the political and social climate.[15]

If the legal system is applied and legal justice enacted, the judge has then carried out the obligation to apply the law in accordance with the rules laid down. The obligation to the legal system is therefore satisfied. The obligation to morality has also been satisfied because the person who broke the moral code has been caught and punished. At this point, however, morality is of further importance. How immoral is the act of blowing up other people's property; how immoral is it to shock members of the community who follow conventional morality? The conclusion may have some bearing on the sentence. Political values also enter at this point, in particular the value of prudence. Is the act isolated or is it part of a larger plot; if the activist receives a long sentence, will the person be made a martyr and therefore further his/her cause; will a long sentence lead to further acts of violence as a way of protest or will it be a deterrent? A careful weighing up of these questions changes a possible sentence of three years to one of six months' imprisonment. Legality and morality have been upheld but prudential considerations have qualified the sentence.

What has happened in this case is that, within a communal form of life as in an individual one, there is a hierarchy of value systems: some value systems in certain instances are considered more important than others. Occasionally only one value system may come into play. For instance, in judging a picture for its beauty, our aesthetic value system may be the only one that is used. Sometimes, however, more than one value system is relevant, and to know a person's form of life will indicate which system will take precedence. Indeed, if we really knew a person's form of life, we would know not only which value system but also which value within a system would take precedence in a conflict.

We are now in a position to see in greater detail when a political system will be valued. It will be valued if it allows us to follow our form of life or if it furthers our form of life. It may be that certain governmental actions offend our moral values but we may accept them because they agree with our prudential value system. On the other hand, they may agree with neither but we still maintain our obligation if governmental actions generally agree with our form of life. Theoretically it seems that three things can disturb this maintenance:

1   Actions are pursued which threaten our form of life.
2   Actions are pursued which are opposed to important values within an important value system in our form of life.
3   Alternative political systems seem more attractive, perhaps because
(a) the political system within which we live generally allows the existence of our form of life but another will actually further it;
(b) our political system does not favour our form of life but another allows the existence of it;
(c) our political system does not favour our form of life but another will further it.

When one has a political obligation to a system, one need not be concerned with every detail of legislation or with political action. However, if legislation or political action continually goes against the contents of one's form of life then one's political obligation begins to waver. In other words, if governmental action indicates that the set-up no longer allows or values the things that one values then quite obviously the value that was inherent in it, and was the grounds for one's obligation, no longer exists. However, this cannot provide a justification for rebellion, as in this case rebellion would be based on the subjective whim of one person, as well as being foolish from a practical point of view.

Under this analysis of the concept of the form of life, if the government on the whole does not favour the communal form of life (communal values), then a general withdrawal of political obligation can take place. In such a case there could be a sufficient justification for a rebellion.

In practice, in spite of the failure of a political system to take note of the communal shared values, we might still decide that it is the best of a bad bunch. We would be ranking it favourably with the others available, even though we graded it against the ideal as of little value. In this case we could have a duty towards it, in conflict with other systems. It could also be the case that, although we think that the system is fairly bad, we nevertheless recognize that there are certain change mechanisms within it that can lead to improvements and so are prepared to give it our allegiance.

Under such an argument, political obligation becomes very personal, and perhaps to the sovereign unimportant, because, although one may not have a political obligation to the system, one will still have a legal obligation to obey the laws. It cannot be successfully argued that one can obey or disobey a particular law depending on whether or not one valued it. If it could then chaos would reign, and a situation similar to a Hobbesian state of nature would exist. One can deny that one has a political obligation to the system but still follow the laws of the state because of other prudential, rational, and moral obligations. However, a withdrawal of political obligation will entail a hypercritical stance, as one will be suspicious of every new law or action of the government. It will also be important in extreme cases because, as we have seen, the continual irrational acts of a pathological government against the shared values of the community can lead to a general withdrawal of political obligation: the vast majority of individuals will no longer have a political obligation to the system. This leaves the legal framework on its own, completely naked, so that it will be clearly seen that the irrational laws of a pathological regime are unprincipled, that they are not derived from the principles of justice inherent in the legal tradition, and that they do not reflect the shared values of the community. This can lead to the claim that the irrational laws are illegal,[16] even though they seem to have been passed by the legitimate procedure. This in its turn leads to the argument that the legal framework itself has become illegitimate and that this rescinds our legal obligation to obey the laws: a situation of rebellion will therefore exist. A general withdrawal of political obligation can therefore withdraw the veil of legitimacy from the legal system and be instrumental in instigating rebellion.

We can thus say that individuals no longer have a political obligation to a system when it no longer values the things that they value, even though they still have a legal obligation to obey its laws. Grounds for rebellion and a withdrawal of legal obligation can be found not when one person but when the vast majority feels that the system no longer preserves or even threatens the existence of their values. In other words, a general withdrawal of political obligation is a refusal to recognize the legitimacy of the regime and is thereby a declaration that the laws of the regime are not true laws, and that therefore there is no legal obligation to obey them.

The analysis has indicated why we value political organizations. It has shown what we mean by saying that we value something, and what we mean by stating that we have a duty or obligation to something.[17] It has also pointed out the relative importance of certain obligations. Most importantly it has indicated that morality lies at the base of government: a government that too often and for too long excessively ignores the values inherent in its own society will inevitably fall. Political education must therefore be mostly concerned with values; being so concerned not only strengthens society but can help to keep a better check on governmental excesses.

CONCLUSION

It is often said that we get the governments that we deserve. This is simply making the point that the social structure which we create will be reflected in the institutional and power structure that governs society. Marx makes this point when he argues that in a class society governments will operate in the interests of the ruling class. Our point is very similar: politics is the articulation of a form of life. A society in which people are generally free to follow their own pursuits without undue interference from others, in which people respect each other as people and therefore their freedoms, requires a certain kind of attitude to be reflected in their institutions. It needs a particular sort of framework which will enable their desires to flourish. The desires are articulated socially by the political society, which in its turn creates the framework and opportunity for a particular form of life. The political society thus has extrinsic worth, since it openly allows us to develop our own moral life.

Political society is like a fragile plant: if we give it too little water, it wilts and dies; if we give it too much water, it rots and dies. In politics, if we are too apathetic and complacent, we can find that our political society has passed on to something else; if we are too vigilant and critical, it can collapse into a mire of bickering and disagreement.

As can be seen, education and politics are entwined. Politics is concerned with the establishment and justification of certain values and with their implementation in society. A political system provides the framework for this activity to take place. Education is concerned not only with the understanding of principles and values and with their justification but also with developing the ability to formulate principles and values, to assess them, and to compare them. It is concerned with developing the ability to make distinctions, to decide whether something is relevant or not. An ideal political system allows the maximum interplay of ideas to take place and avoids violence. An ideal educational system likewise maximizes the ability of people to participate in the political process.

Chapter three

TEACHING, LEARNING, AND LIBERAL EDUCATION

In developing the arguments in this chapter, we are really exploring some of the assumptions made by a group of writers on the nature of education. We can classify these writers as liberal educators, who include in their ideas a vision of the intellectual achievement of human beings, of the intellectual power and progress of humans as almost demi-gods. They perceive how this power is obtained and developed but their very analysis of the nature of knowledge leads them to recognize that, in practice, each step in its acquisition can only be faltering, and that the vision of human beings is only a vision. It is part of a form of life that is desirable but never achievable. In a sense it is the intellectualization of the power game and is an essential part of the mode of politics.

VALUES, FACTS, AND POINTS OF VIEW

It has often been asserted that rational argument is based on the revelation of facts, and that disputes, if they are to remain rational, must also be concerned with the nature of the facts. In other words, if the facts are properly understood by the disputants in the argument, then the argument and disagreement should end. If the dispute continues after there has been agreement on all of the facts, then the conclusion must be that the dispute can be based only on the prejudice of the disputants. Clearly, if two disputants agree on all of the facts and the dispute continues, then one cannot persuade the other to change opinion by reference to the facts because they will already have been taken into account. For instance, if there is a dispute between A and B, and they have factual agreement on a to z, and then A tries to persuade B that what A proposes is justified by a, b, c, we have the problem that B has already taken a, b, c into account when reaching a conclusion. It would therefore not be possible to persuade B to change opinion by reference to a, b, c. The disagreement must thus be based on values and not facts and, if so, it must be based on irrational feeling or emotions, i.e. prejudice.

This sort of argument raises problems for ethical and political discourse because, as we have seen, much argument in this area is concerned with values and not facts. The question arises as to whether non-factual arguments are based on mere prejudice. If they are, then any change in the beliefs of the disputants, over and above belief about the facts, will not be on rational grounds. A settlement of such a dispute can come about only by force, by the threat of force, by one side shouting down the other, or by some other persuasive method.

To counter this argument, we must demonstrate that disputes can continue on rational grounds, even if there is agreement on the facts. An obvious example is when we engage in a dispute about a piece of literature or philosophy. In this case the texts are available (that is, we agree on the facts) but we argue about how the text should be interpreted. Our disagreement is not mere prejudice but concerns the meaning of a particular part of a text, which may have a fundamental influence on our understanding of the text as a whole. We are suggesting that it is possible to look at accepted facts in a new and perhaps deeper way and to bring to the surface new meanings. Of course, it should be possible to show someone the basis for the new interpretation and deeper meaning, which indicates that facts are not just facts but must be regarded in a certain way in order to have their meaning extracted. Rational discourse and disagreement can continue to take place even though we agree on all of the facts.

The notion of looking at facts in a new way provides the basis for a second example. Suppose we desire to hang a picture on a wall but, unfortunately, we find that we do not possess a hammer to enable us to bang a nail into the wall on which to hang it. We then look round the room for something that we can use as a hammer; our gaze falls on a suitable shoe that we can use. Here we have recognized the properties required by a hammer to be effective and have seen that the shoe also has the necessary properties for our purpose. Of course, the shoe is seen as a potential hammer only when we are looking around for such an object, within the context of 'hammerability'. In a more general sense, we are looking at the shoe in the framework of a useful performance of the specific task of hammering the nail into the wall. The example is teleological, as we are aiming at a specific end. Again, we are going beyond the fact that the shoe is a shoe and are suggesting that there is a new use for it.

A third example is the case of a doctor who makes a diagnosis. The doctor will not be concerned with every physical and mental attribute of a patient but with facts that are relevant for making a diagnosis. In other words, the doctor is concerned with symptoms and tries to fit the symptoms into a pattern, so that they may be recognized as symptoms of a certain disease, and in so doing makes a diagnosis.[1] (It is true that this example is also teleological, because the doctor is concerned with the future treatment of the patient, but this is only a contingent fact, since the diagnosis could be made whether or not the doctor intended to treat the patient and could be judged to be either correct or incorrect, irrespective of the treatment.)

The above examples have been given in order to demonstrate that rational discourse can continue, even when the facts are agreed on and yet a dispute continues. In the first example, the dispute, in spite of textual agreement, is about interpretation; in the second example, it concerns whether or not a particular object is useful for a practical activity; in the third example, it relates to whether a particular pattern of symptoms can form the basis of a correct diagnosis. We are not arguing that facts are irrelevant. In the textual example, the new interpretation, in order to have any chance of being acceptable, must explain the facts (the text) in a new light, i.e. it cannot ignore the text. The facts must be consistent with the new interpretation. In the case of the hammer, the shoe must at least be seen to have the properties of a hammer (a soft-heeled slipper would be of no use), so that it can be successfully used to bring about the practical result of knocking the nail into the wall. In the medical example, the symptoms must be consistent with a particular diagnosis in order to have any credibility, i.e. the symptoms as facts must fit into the range of symptoms usually associated with a particular disease.

It can also be seen that, in the hammer and the medical

examples, we can look at the same facts from a completely different point of view. For instance, we might admire a small statue from an aesthetic viewpoint and be concerned with its beauty or we might look at it from a utilitarian viewpoint and consider whether we could use it to bang a nail into a wall. Similarly, we might either admire the beauty of the human body or be concerned with the diagnosis of a disease. Certain features of a particular object are given their significance because of the way in which we consider them. If we look at an object from a particular point of view, we will consider it in a different way and make different judgements about it than if we looked at it from another point of view.

If we judge something from a particular viewpoint, we are judging it according to the standards appropriate to that viewpoint. It is these standards which lead us to recognize that certain facts are important from one point of view but not from another. We may consider facts to be neutral until we give them meaning by looking at them from a particular viewpoint. For example, take the case of an old woman walking down the street with a handbag over her shoulder. Suddenly a car draws up beside her and the bag is snatched away. She is pushed over. The thief leaps back into the car, which then rapidly disappears into the distance. We might look at the event from a technical viewpoint and consider the cleverness and efficiency of the robbery, or we might look at it from the moral point of view and consider its iniquity. From a technical point of view its iniquity is irrelevant; from the moral point of view its efficiency has nothing to do with the case. In other words, we would be making an appraisal from different viewpoints and therefore taking into account different standards. It follows that different features of the happening would be relevant for our consideration, and that the neutral facts would have been given meaning by reference to the different standards appropriate to the different points of view.

A similar insight into our organization of the world of neutral facts has been taken up and developed by a number of philosophers who believe that we attempt to organize the whole of experience in a way not unlike the way that we have suggested. In a sense, we create a system of ideas so that we can give meaning to the world around us. It can be argued that our experience is really a collection of ideas that we have about the world, and that we begin to understand the world when we organize that experience. We attempt to create stability out of chaos, a stability which is more satisfactory and understandable to us than the real world. In order to achieve stability, our ultimate aim must be the achievement of coherence in our experience, in the collection of ideas.

At this point, one may wonder where truth is if we create the collection of ideas. Truth must be related to the concept of coherence but remember, as shown in our examples, that it is also related to the neutral facts. They cannot be ignored. The argument entails that it is not really possible to separate the real world from our experience of it. Our experience appears as a world of ideas which we organize and communicate to others. In that sense, attempting to understand the world and giving it meaning, we are indicating that the real world is rational and that we can be objective. To say that something has meaning means that we can understand it and that our understanding enables us to communicate its meaning to others. By putting our understanding into the public arena we are opening it to debate and criticism and are declaring its objectivity.

However, if our ultimate aim is to create a coherent world of ideas, which is rational and is therefore capable of being understood not only by ourselves but by others, it is a very tall order. It surely must be the task of the philosopher, in the most metaphysical of moods, to create a system of thought which can explain everything. In practice, this is avoided and we construct and examine the world in restricted ways.

MODES OF EXPERIENCE AND INTERPRETATIVE FRAMEWORKS

Michael Oakeshott calls these restricted ways 'modes of experience'.[2] They are developed as homogeneous and specific pictures of experience from different points of view. They are really restricted attempts to give a coherent view of the world and, as they are from different viewpoints, they are independent of each other.[3] Oakeshott gives us four obvious examples: practice, science, history, and poetry.

As each mode is independent, we can consider it to be autonomous, with no direct relationship with another. Each looks at the world in a different way, having developed its own language and logic. It is therefore not possible to speak of disputes or disagreements between the different modes. Indeed, to use the language and logic of one mode in another mode can lead only to confusion because the language, although it may appear to be the same, will have developed different meanings and connotations. For instance, although technology and science are apparently connected, what is relevant to one may be irrelevant to the other. Technology is concerned with practice, efficiency, and cost, whereas science is concerned with none of these things. Science examines the world under the category of quantity and is therefore mainly concerned with measurement. It develops systematic and coherent ideas related to this task and also the specialized language needed to exchange ideas amongst the cognoscenti. The mode is autonomous, in the sense that truth claims will be related to its coherence and that other ways of looking at the world will be irrelevant to it.

This way of looking at our organization of experience seems quite fruitful. In history we can see a number of attempts to develop a systematic way of looking at the world which lose their way because they become mixed up with other ways of looking at the world. For instance, in the work of some utilitarians, attempts have been made to develop a morality based on a scientific methodology. Thus, Jeremy Bentham argues that the only good is pleasure and the only evil pain, and that both of these feelings can be measured. Also, the Marxist historian confuses the historical mode with the mode of practice and believes that one can use a knowledge of history to bring about good results.

We can consciously create modes of experience by carefully making distinctions between ways of looking at experiences and differentiating one approach from another. For instance, over the years attempts have been made to distinguish between the law and morality. A legal positivist would argue that, although similar language is used in both law and morality, the validity of the law has nothing to do with morality. The analysis in Chapter 2 of political obligation and political values goes some way to deny such attempts and is also a denial of the autonomy of law.

We have really looked at our experience in a highly theoretical way, by developing a general theory about how the world is experienced, but we still need a more dynamic theory to explain how we actually understand it. How do we form our understanding of the world? Michael Polanyi, in his writings, suggests at least the basis for such a theory.[4] It is his ideas that we intend to explore and develop. The concepts of the interpretative framework and tacit knowledge seem to be of great importance in this respect.

An interpretative framework is a systematic way of looking at the world that creates order and gives stability to our understanding. We examine things from the viewpoint of an interpretative framework so that we can understand and make judgements about them. A good example of an interpretative framework is that of Marxism. Certain features of the framework are well known. To illustrate what we mean we will develop a caricature of such a framework. Each society will be a class society, the ruling class will control the means of production, the state will be used by the ruling class to retain its power. The state will have a parasitic element in it, so a bureaucracy will develop which will also tend to do things in its own interests. The rising class will be on the side of progress but, when it comes to power, will itself be a fetter to progress, and so on. Each part of the framework will fit together with the rest. In this sense, an attempt will be made to make the whole theory systematic, coherent and, importantly, flexible. When a particular situation is studied, it will be investigated from the point of view of the framework. The framework will tell the researcher what to look for and will indicate what is relevant and what is not. The process of research will therefore tend to confirm the validity of the approach; contradictory evidence will tend to be considered not as a direct challenge to the interpretation but as grounds for improving its sophistication.

In practice, therefore, conflict will be understood to be class conflict, evidence will be found to indicate that the ruling class rules in its own interest, and so on. Even language will be carefully used to avoid challenging the framework. For instance, Marx, when examining the reign of Louis Philippe, King of the French, finds that the ruling class, the bourgeoisie as a whole, are not ruling as they should be in orthodox theory.[5] In order to cope with this discrepancy, Marx calls the competing groups from the same class 'factions of the ruling class' and not different classes. This he had to do if he was going to retain the coherence of his position. At a more fundamental level, Lenin copes with the fact that capitalism has failed to collapse by developing his theory of imperialism; at a later date we get the development of the theory of economic imperialism. Ad hoc additions are made in order to preserve the framework and to make it more flexible. The integrity and coherence of the framework is maintained in spite of the fact that certain anomalies seem to have emerged. (They are explained away.)

The very process of thinking involves making judgements and judgements can be understood only by looking at them in the context of different frameworks of ideas.[6] There seem to be four possibilities when making a judgement:

1   A correct judgement in a correct interpretative framework.
2   An incorrect judgement in a correct interpretative framework.
3   A correct judgement in an incorrect interpretative framework.
4   An incorrect judgement in an incorrect interpretative framework.

All judgements must take place within an interpretative framework and can be understood and assessed only by reference to it. An interpretative framework is a way of looking at things in order to give some stability to our perceptions. It can be argued that we fit things into a framework so that we can understand and make judgements about them. Of course, following this line of thought, we could also have neither judgement nor interpretative framework. However, this would be introducing new criteria and therefore should be distinguished from the possibilities that arose within a framework. We thus have four possibilities (++, -+, +-, --). The fifth possibility is not of the same sequence; for instance, it would apply to non-thinking animals, e.g. rats with part of their brains removed.

The relationships between modes of experience, points of view, and interpretative frameworks need to be worked out. The concepts of a point of view and of a mode of experience seem to be close. Perhaps we could say that a point of view is a way of looking at the world but a mode of experience is a way of organizing the world more systematically. We can take science as a mode of experience.

In science we look at things from a restricted point of view and attempt to look at the world under the category of quantity. We are therefore concerned with measurement. The world of ideas which we create has certain features. It is stable, uniform, and common, which enables us to communicate its contents to others. Personal perceptions, intuitions, and feelings may be necessary in the process of discovery but they will be withdrawn in order to achieve communicability, public knowledge. The most communicable and stable language is the mathematical language of measurement. Indeed, if our scientific ideas cannot be put in terms of mathematical relationships, we can consider our ideas to be non-scientific or at least pre-scientific.

When we look at phenomena from a particular mode of experience, we may well use different frameworks to organize them. It is possible that these interpretative frameworks will also be incommensurable, having their own special language and concepts, e.g. Lamarckianism and Neo-Darwinism, or the physics of Newton and Einstein. Nevertheless, the mode of experience will determine in a very general way what is relevant and what is not. For instance, science continues to look at things under the category of quantity (being concerned with measurement and the finding of causal relations), even though it may use different ways of organizing an experience.

TACIT KNOWLEDGE

This discussion about modes of experience and inter-pretative frameworks is of the utmost importance for education, as it indicates what pupils need to do if they are going to be considered at all educated. They need to develop the ability to distinguish one point of view or mode of experience from another. They will eventually need to understand different modes of experience and interpretative frameworks and to be able to use the appropriate language in the right way within the modes and frameworks. Ultimately, the aim of the process of education is to develop the skill of a connoisseur and an ability to make independent judgements on the part of a pupil. Clearly this is a tremendous task and one which few pupils can achieve. Of course, we could pitch our target at a lower level and argue that an educated person should perhaps be an expert in one mode and have some knowledge of the language and means of approach of others. In doing so, we may make room for ourselves but will lose the grandeur of the ultimate intellectual aim of education (really of liberal education): to create the complete Renaissance figure, a polymath.

Of course, this way of thinking about education relates education to the concept of power, to a desire to be omniscient. Interestingly, Michael Polanyi defines education thus: 'Education is latent knowledge, of which we are aware subsidiarily in our sense of intellectual power based on this knowledge.'[7] He means by this that we cannot be certain of the extent of our knowledge. It is not something that we can wear on our sleeve, continually exposed. It is something that we know we possess, rather by our awareness of our own mastery of the subject matter in question than by our immediate awareness of all of the items of knowledge contained within that mastery. In this sense, education can be thought of as power, a power to control one's subject. In the intellectual sphere it would mean that we had developed the conceptual power and ability to recognize instances of the things that we know, and the ability to go beyond this to recognize new instances and to fit them into our framework of knowledge. We would have the ability to bring stability to these new instances by rejecting their randomness and by controlling them by fitting them into our framework. We would therefore have the ability to make them understandable to ourselves and, ultimately, to others.

This is a dynamic concept of education because it is a matter not of assimilating information but of taking in information, understanding it, and developing the ability to use it. Further, it is not a passive notion, whereby we develop all of the abilities and wait for the problems to arise, but is achievement-oriented, whereby we look for problems and attempt to solve them. In doing so, we increase our control over things previously unknown. Indeed, it can be argued that it is the mark of the educated mind to be thus achievement-oriented. By continually searching out and solving new problems, and by understanding new experiences, we widen our knowledge base and gradually modify the framework of our understanding.

Michael Polanyi has developed a concept which is important for our understanding of the nature of education. It is the concept of tacit knowledge. He argues that all of our explicit knowledge exists within a tacit framework, by which he means that it is surrounded by a whole body of known and unknown assumptions that give rise to our explicit knowledge and give it context and meaning. This provides the framework for our judgement. Of course, it is possible to make some of our tacit knowledge known, i.e. explicit, but the argument is that we can never make known all of our knowledge. If we try to analyse it, we begin to recognize that it is based on a regression of assumptions.

The concept of tacit knowledge points to some interesting insights into education and raises a number of questions about the nature of our understanding and the status of our knowledge.

On knowledge

The concept of tacit knowledge indicates that we can never be certain that we are correct in our knowledge claims, since they are always fuzzy-edged as our explicit knowledge fades into its tacit framework. To claim that we know is a matter of judgement on our part and, although we may feel that our judgement is correct and so are committed to it, is always open to argument and debate.

The recognition that our knowledge is fuzzy-edged and merges into our non-expressed and inexpressible commitments and prejudices means that, in order to communicate with others and to be understood by them, we must develop a public language in which to express our ideas. We must put our arguments in a form that will allow public debate, that is, be as objective as possible.

An attempt to be objective indicates a commitment to the truth and a recognition that it is very easy to rely on our prejudices. It is an intellectual achievement which allows public debate.

The concept of objectivity also leads us to recognize that knowledge exists within a social context, i.e. within a public debate. Knowledge claims or truth claims are assessed in the public debate and it is the public (consisting of other experts) that gives, or fails to give, the claims the status of truth.

The public can be wrong in its assessment, since the knowledge by which it judges truth claims is also fuzzy-edged. The public will compare new claims with accepted knowledge and, of course, accepted knowledge can be wrong. The public debate in this sense is never completely closed.

On teaching and learning

As experts know more than they can tell, they realize that they can pass on more than they can make explicit. They can do this by showing pupils how to look at the world in a certain way, for instance, how to look at it in the way of the art expert; how to develop the knowledge, skills, and abilities of the expert; how to make judgements and to develop and present arguments in the way appropriate to the subject matter in question; how to engage in a public debate with other experts.

As teachers, the experts are able to instruct the pupils in explicit knowledge, i.e. they can give chunks of information but they are also able to impart abilities, including the ability to make judgements. Abilities and the capacity to make judgements are picked up by the practice of the pupils and by their attempts to make judgements, and also by watching and copying the experts. The pupils will have to take much on trust, since they have neither the skill nor the knowledge to challenge the experts. Over a period of time they will learn not only information but also a vast array of skills, judgements and methods, which will become part of the basis for making their own judgements and decisions in later life. They will form a vast framework of subsidiary knowledge on which they can base their judgements.

On the structure of knowing

Polanyi actually sketches out how the dynamic process of knowing comes about. He calls it a process of 'tacit integration'.[8] This integration happens when we attend from one set of objects to another. It has a from-to structure. We use subsidiary knowledge, knowledge that we are not looking at in itself, to attend to focal knowledge, something we wish to make explicit. We take the subsidiary knowledge as given and do not examine it or criticize it, and then attend to something else. In a sense, therefore, subsidiary knowledge has a functional relationship to focal knowledge.

There is necessarily a tacit component in all knowledge, a component that can never be completely revealed. Thus we cannot be entirely aware of the many facets of our own understanding and so, for instance, we cannot be completely aware of all of the dimensions of our interpretative framework, the influence of our peer group, or the influence of our own feelings or prejudices.

It can be seen that education is a continuing process: we react to debate and argument, and accept and reject different judgements. It is a process of continually widening the base of our knowledge so that we can more successfully bring it to bear on new problems. It gives us a certain degree of mastery and control over our future and, as has been argued, is in that sense the acquisition of power.

Judgements come about when we begin to concentrate on a problem, to focus the vast array of subsidiary knowledge on that problem. We immerse ourselves in the problem and gradually move towards a solution. The immersion is not only intellectual but also emotional, since it is making use of the skills, knowledge, and prejudices that we have acquired, which have become an extension of our own mind/body.[9]

On being a person

It is sometimes asked whether teaching is really concerned with initiating pupils into an inheritance of human achievement, or whether it is designed to enable pupils to make the most of themselves. Michael Oakeshott suggests that such a question is really inappropriate because the pupils learn to make the most of themselves by living in a world of human achievement.[10] We wish to explore this thought.

Self-consciousness seems to lie at the base of human achievement, as it is only when we become conscious of ourselves that we begin to recognize our own individuality and to separate ourselves from other people. The recognition of ourselves as a separate person leads us to explore our own nature and then to compare ourselves with other beings. We begin to see what we are and what we can be, and begin to see that we can succeed in our aims and that we can fail. We begin to recognize what ideally we could be, and what we ought to be. In doing this we look at others and at the relationships that we have and can have with them. We are really beginning to develop a morality, since we are examining human beings in an abstract way. We are looking at humans in their universal aspect and considering what it means to be human. It can be seen that the development of morality is an intellectual achievement arising out of our self-awareness. For instance, we can argue that the principle 'treat others as you would wish to be treated' is a universalization of the respect that we have for ourselves. It is a recognition that other individuals are like ourselves and therefore should be treated in the same way as ourselves.

We can argue that our own recognition of our nature and the like nature of others lies at the heart of intellectual attainment. It is a recognition that our own understanding of beings and objects can be compared with that of other people, and that we can use other people's understanding to contrast with and check our own understanding. Our ability to communicate our beliefs to others and their ability to understand and to recommunicate is the basis of human achievement and objectivity. The very fact that we can talk about, for instance, our appreciation of beauty or our understanding of the environment indicates that we are attempting to be objective. Of course, as we develop from a normal appreciation of beauty to a deeper understanding of art and literature, or as we move from just looking at trees and insects to their classification, we develop a whole array of rules, standards, techniques, and meanings. We are really developing coherent but intellectualized ways of looking at the world.

The whole world of intellectual achievement has arisen out of our original desire to understand ourselves and others. It is created by a heuristic passion, desire to find the truth, to discover, to understand, and thereby ultimately to control.

To initiate children into the 'literature of civilization' is not just attempting to get them to understand and to use the languages of the way in which we look at the world but is leading them to discover their own talents, and to recognize themselves and their abilities. A major function of education is thus to lead children to a self-knowledge, since only through this self-knowledge can they properly understand not only themselves but other people and other things. It is also allowing them to catch a glimpse of, and perhaps participate in, the whole field of human achievement.

Human achievement is a social achievement, and arises from a coming together to understand, appreciate, and control the world. It is also, as we have seen, an intellectual achievement that has arisen from our ability to recognize ourselves, to distinguish things, and to decide what is relevant to our understanding and what is not.

LIBERAL EDUCATION AND POLITICS

We have argued that human achievement is a social achievement. This can best be seen in the development of different intellectual communities which control different subject disciplines. In order to develop our argument further, we will look briefly at the structure of such communities and in particular at Polanyi's paradigm example of such a community, the 'Republic of Science'.[11]

The community is governed by mature scientists, that is, by scientists who have developed their own contact with reality. Polanyi denies that there is a hierarchy of authority within the community because he claims that the mature scientists exercise a mutual authority, an authority where they are the recognized authority. Thus mature scientists, because they are the recognized authorities in the discipline, the experts, are in authority and mutually make up the decision procedure of the community.

These scientists judge innovations by reference to the knowledge that they already possess. Polanyi envisages a network of knowledge where scientists' knowledge overlaps with other scientists' knowledge. When a discovering scientist makes a truth claim, the community spontaneously comes to a decision through the operation of its network of knowledge.

It can be seen that the community is bound by the traditions of the community, not only by the interpersonal knowledge of the community (the network of knowledge) but also by the methods of science and by the skills and abilities of the scientists. An innovation must therefore be seen to fit into the interpersonal knowledge and the method of arriving at the innovation must also be seen to have been followed.

The mode of experience being followed is that of science, so things are being examined under the category of quantity and all mature scientists are judging the proposed innovation from very similar interpretative frameworks. Likewise, the innovator must also be looking at phenomena from a similar interpretative framework. If not, they will simply not understand each other.

The truth claim of the innovator will be based on deep research. The innovator will be committed to the claim but nevertheless it will be fuzzy-edged. It will be put before the community for acceptance but, as we have seen, the interpersonal knowledge by which they will judge it is also fuzzy-edged. Nevertheless, the community of scientists will decide on its acceptability. They can decide whether or not to give the claim the status of truth. The truth badge can be given or withdrawn depending on whether or not the innovation meets the criteria set up by the community: it has the quality of defeasibility.[12]

However, even if the community refuses to accept the

innovation, the innovator could well be justified in continuing to uphold it, in gaining more evidence, and attempting to persuade other scientists to be allies. After all, neither the innovator's truth claim nor the knowledge of the community is certain, and both the innovating scientist and the community can make mistakes. The innovator will have to argue the case in the public language of science and to follow the conventions of scientific objectivity. The debate itself will be free and open, with the hope that the truth will out. This is really the argument that a free and open debate is the most likely procedure to achieve the truth. The innovative scientist also accepts the right of the scientific community to make the decision as to the worth of the innovation. It is the legitimate decision procedure.

The community is also bound together by mutual obligations derived from the original obligation to seek and reveal the truth. The community cannot function unless there is professional integrity and honesty: an obligation to transcendent values.

Interestingly, we can see that this analysis of the paradigm example of an academic community is remarkably similar to the ideal liberal community developed by liberal writers, for instance, J.S. Mill in On Liberty and Karl Popper in The Open Society and Its Enemies. Indeed, Polanyi uses his analysis of the scientific community as a prototype model which he sketchily develops into a study of the political community.[13] The belief in human achievement, in progress, in truth, in the openness of discussion, in universal participation, with responsible freedom within a developing tradition, is characteristic of liberal thought. Michael Oakeshott, in his own analysis of politics, is the odd man out. He is reluctant to see the pursuit of politics as analogous to an academic community searching for the truth. Its traditions are not systematic and politics is concerned with keeping the system on the rails - the conversation going - rather than with any attempt to arrive at the truth.

Nevertheless, we believe that the concept of politics, as generally expressed in the writings of Polanyi, Popper, Oakeshott, Crick, Porter, and Stradling, is a concept of politics closely tied in with the whole concept of liberal education. It is an expression of the same form of life as liberal education, which includes a particular way of looking at nature and the intellectual world and which has struggled for dominance in the last three centuries of Western culture. It is very much tied in with the notion of man as an achiever; an intellect concerned with the universalization of concepts, with the secularization of man as a fragment of God, with the notion of man as the moral legislator. Liberal education is the educational face of this vision of man as an achieving intellect. Politics in this special sense is the intellectualized face of the democracy of this autonomous achiever.

Chapter four

THE POLITICAL COMMUNITY

In this chapter we look at some of the characteristics of a political community. It is not intended to be an all-embracing examination but deals with essential features and points to some areas for discussion and debate. It also prepares the ground for Chapter 6, on the curriculum for a programme of political education. We cannot begin to consider what should be contained in such a curriculum until we develop some agreement about the contents of politics.

We have argued that the idea of a liberal education is tied up with a particular notion of a political being who desires a particular form of life. A political community provides the conditions that allow this form of life to exist. In looking at the framework for a political being's existence, we shall not be indulging in the development of unattainable Utopia but will be formulating, in an abstract way, an idealized version of actuality. We are asking what it means to act ethically or morally (the analysis suggests a difference) in the political sphere. We are asking whether a political set-up can reflect the essentials of a form of life that we have created, by thinking about the relation of people, one to another, and that we can contrast with actuality. In a sense, it can be considered an intellectual-ization of our more sordid and mundane lives. Political education is bound to provide a running critique of our everyday life and institutions, since it brings to mind what we hope to achieve and emphasizes the moral approach. However, it is not fundamentally a revolutionary procedure because it is a drawing out of concepts and intimations that already exist in our everyday life. The political model is thus not just another model or ideology but a rational model derived from a Western liberal point of view. In some ways it is a model which would be equally acceptable to John

Stuart Mill and to Karl Marx but whereas one might say that our society is something like it, the other would say it is nothing like it.

This, of course, is the fundamental dilemma for a government that contemplates encouraging political education. On the one hand, from the point of view of a person in the hurly-burly of actual politics, it is useful to encourage an understanding of the intellectual idea of a political community; on the other hand, its revelation may well lead to discontent with our earthly lot. However, politics and ethics are concerned with practice, with how we act socially and individually on this earth. They are intellectualizations of our practice rather than the creation of heavenly bodies.

It is clear that politics is concerned with the government of a complex and sophisticated society, with a form of government that has been thought about and adapted to suit circumstances. It is unlikely that a political society will just emerge, since it includes sophisticated notions about the nature and role of individuals and their relationship with others and with their government. A political society will include power relations but not exclusively. Political societies are conscious creations which have emerged after many centuries of conflict and argument. The form of emergence has been greatly influenced by the mulling over of ideas about justice, the exercise of authority, and citizenship.

It can be argued that power comes first, and that the rest is merely an attempt to legitimate the power relations between the participants in the community. For example, following a conquest, we see the emergence of notions about kingship; rules are designed, setting out the relationship of the king to his own supporters and to the conquered, and perhaps even to God. The rules not only legitimize his authority but also limit that authority and thereby regularize his power. The rules create stability by attempting to regulate policy and by helping to prevent the arbitrary exercise of power. Eventually power can be legitimately exercised only by the authority designated by the rules. The rules are conscious creations, setting out how an association of people can live together, and politics emerges from this conscious and continual consideration.

A number of points have arisen from the above discussion. When people associate, they begin to stabilize their relationship by establishing rules, and de facto power develops into de jure authority. The rules are concerned with the regulation of conduct, and the rules themselves must be appropriate for the situation in question. In practice, they have to reflect the power relations that exist but they have to do more: their function is to raise the situation from the sphere of naked power towards regular authority. There needs to be agreement that the rules developed are appropriate for the circumstances and therefore acceptable. Of course, rules can be acceptable for a number of reasons and need not be rational. For instance, they could reflect a tradition or the idiosyncrasy of some leader. However, if rules are going to be maintained and respected, there must be some public agreement that they are acceptable.

A further characteristic of rules concerned with regulating human conduct is that they are bound to be normative and will prescribe certain standards of conduct. They will state what a person or insitution can and cannot do, what is correct and incorrect and, in more sophisticated societies, what is legal and illegal. The rules, of course, do not determine what action will take place, as they are not scientific rules, but they must be taken into account by people and institutions when actions are being considered. A feature of a normative rule is that it is humanly created and is therefore the product of people living within social situations. Normative rules exist because people have willed them to exist; they can exist only as long as people continue to will them into existence. However, if rules are to exist and to have influence on people's lives, any obstructions to and infractions of the rules must be negated. Thus rules must not only be willed into continued existence but also supported by sanctions.

Bernard Crick argues that 'the establishing of political order is not just any order at all; it marks the birth or recognition of freedom',[1] but it is a special sort of freedom closely connected to the establishment of rules. In a political community we find the acceptance of a plurality of interests, groups, and traditions, which exist together within a designated geographical area under a common rule. If notice is going to be taken of these differing interests, groups, and traditions, opportunities must be given for their different points of view to be expressed. Freedom of speech must be a basic requirement for such an order. However, as J.S. Mill has pointed out, the process of government is not just concerned with expressing and discussing opinions and different points of view. It must make decisions and conduct actions. In practice this means that a decision procedure has to be established and that it is a necessary feature of all political communities. Of course, the form of the decision procedure may vary from community to community. Indeed, we are able to identify the type of community by examining the formal and informal structure of the decision procedure. We can undertake an examination of the processess that lead up to decisions, since it is here that we can see whether or not freedom for discussion and argument operates. The actual decisions taken may limit freedom by establishing rules that forbid citizens to undertake certain actions but may, nevertheless, allow a greater degree of freedom to law-abiding citizens. J.S. Mill also argued:

> All that makes existence valuable to anyone depends on the enforcement of restraints upon the actions of other people. Some rules of conduct, therefore, be imposed by law in the first place, and by opinion on many things which are not fit subjects for the operation of law.[2]

The Rule of Law is an essential feature of any free society. The law indicates what a person can and cannot do. It sets out the area of individual freedom, as it tells individuals where their liberty lies, and protects them from the interference of others in their legitimate pursuit.

The law also protects individuals from the arbitrary fiats of the sovereign. If they obey the law, they will not be punished by the ruler's power. This is an essential feature of the Rule of Law, since, if they were not protected in this way, they would be in the same position as slaves who are liable to punishment on the mere whim of their master. The Rule of Law is thus a necessary feature of a free society but the extent of freedom will depend on how far the law extends, and to what degree a citizen has participated in its enactment.

The ideal political community will have within it citizens rather than subjects. A subject needs only to know the law and to obey but citizens need to know how to rule as well or, on a lower plane, need to take on some of the responsibilities of government.

Aristotle stated: 'Ruling and obeying are two different things, but the good citizen ought to be capable of both, civic virtue consists in knowing how to govern like a freeman and how to obey like a freeman.'[3]

As a citizen, a person will have certain rights but also certain duties in relation to other people and to the community as a whole but will express citizenship more actively in the civic virtue. Civic virtue consists in being aware of the public debate, in expressing opinions and influencing the body politic, and in pursuing the public interest. It is in this sense that we can have political education which leads pupils to acquire the necessary knowledge and skills to set them on the path to develop and exercise their skill in the furtherance of the public interest. The most politically virtuous will feasibly also develop the arts of persuasion, manipulation, management, and government.

Aristotle, of course, was talking about the ideal city state and it is in such a state that the idea of civic virtue is most intelligible. He argues that there should be equality amongst the citizens but that, nevertheless, the rulers should be drawn from only a small section of citizens: 'Men of good birth are more truly citizens than the low born.'[4]

The idea of citizenship is useful for a concept of democracy but how realistic is it to apply the idea to a modern, multi-cultured, representative democracy?

Behind the notion of representative government is a recognition that only a few will be active in politics. Nevertheless, it is also based on the notion that many will actually be aware of and show an interest in politics, and that there will be many opportunities to express opinions and influence government. Political education can apply only to people who are potential citizens, who are free in the sense that a citizen is free, as Bernard Crick argues: 'Politics are the public actions of free men.'[5]

The ideal of a citizen having political virtue is important, as it points to someone who is active in politics and has concern for the public interest, but the very notion of citizenship has an ethical base. It is based on the notion that the major attribute of man is his rationality; as the Stoics argued, man participates in the rational force that controls the universe, he is a fragment of the cosmos. As all people share in this rationality they are all equal in the sense that they are all, to a degree, rational; however, this very attribute of rationality means that they can make choices, and that they are therefore free. Likewise, in sharing in this rationality, they are sharing in something that is characteristic of the whole of humanity. They have fraternal relations and live in a universal society. The ideas of the Stoics, and particularly of Zeno, are reiterated in the cry of the French Revolution: 'Liberté, égalité, fraternité'. The idea is also picked up again in Kant's notion that human beings, as rational agents, should be treated as an end in themselves and not as a means to an end. However, we do not need to assume that people are equal in their political acumen; all we need to argue is that in order to show a proper respect for a person as a human being, we should allow that person to participate in decisions and give him as much freedom as is commensurate with the freedom of others. Thus, we see the basis for the two-pronged liberal attack against too much governmental interference: against the enforcement of morals, since people, as rational adults, should be able to make their own choices and hold their own beliefs, and against paternalism, since people, who are rational adults, should not be treated as children, i.e. as non-rational agents.

The Stoic stance and the revolutionary cry for liberty, equality, and fraternity point to world government but the concepts of politics and of citizenship point to a limitation of the ethical ideal. In order to explore this limitation, we shall distinguish between general rights and special rights.[6]

GENERAL RIGHTS AND SPECIAL RIGHTS

The argument that there are general rights which apply throughout the world is difficult to substantiate. However, if there are such things, we can say certain things about them. They would have universal application and therefore would apply to everyone. Presumably it could then be claimed that, since we argue that human beings have a special status as unique rational agents or we at least give them the honorary status of being such beings, we should treat them humanely. Perhaps we could argue, as Hobbes does, that if we were going to admit any universal rights at all then we should admit the fundamental and inalienable right of self-preservation, i.e. humans have a right to life. We should also need to argue that all other rights and duties would be derived from such a right. However, if we were going to have any chance of substantiating such a claim, we should also have to argue that these general rights existed prior to man entering civil society, i.e. that they are natural rights and that the function of the state is to protect those rights (a manoeuvre which, for instance, Locke and Hobbes use). There is an alternative, however, and this would be an argument based on pure ethics. We shall return to this later, as it is an alternative that the traditional, natural-law theorists were reaching for but eventually failed to obtain with the argument that their law was neither natural nor lawful.

Special rights, on the other hand, are restricted and apply to people who have developed a special relationship or who have undertaken special transactions amongst themselves. In order to illustrate this notion of special rights, we shall take the case of a teacher who promises her pupils that if they produce an essay by a certain date then, whatever its qualities, they will receive a mark of at least fifty per cent. By making such a promise, the teacher has created for herself the obligation to carry out that promise, and the pupils have the right, providing they do produce the essay on time, to receive a fifty per cent mark. Rights and obligations are really opposite sides of the same coin. Notice, however, how the rights and obligations are limited. The obligation of the teacher is limited to the pupils to whom she made the promise. She has an obligation to no one else. The pupils' right is also limited, since it is a right against that particular teacher and no one else. We can look at communities and argue that their members have a similar relationship, except that they are made up of a mutuality of such rights and obligations, which arise because the members of such communities have inherited special relationships or have undertaken special transactions with each other. The mutual rights and duties are limited to people who have these relationships or have undertaken such transactions. In such a sense, justice lies in the maintenance of such relationships and transactions. It lies in keeping one's agreements. It would seem also that such relationships overrule any general rights that one may have, although Hobbes would presumably argue that one would never enter a relationship that threatened one's life; if one did, it must be void, that is, one always retains the right to self-preservation. (However, consider Socrates' argument in Plato's Crito, whereby one's duty to the city would overrule such a right.) Contract theorists are the most obvious political theorists who make use of such an idea. In a dispute they produce the contract and examine it to see what has been agreed and what has not been agreed. A contract has been made, certain obligations have been incurred and, if one is sensible in the exchange, certain rights have been returned or gained.

In practice, few states have constitutions based on contracts but the argument does not fall. It can be argued that, although there are no written contracts, we can assume that people have developed contract-like relationships by their conventional and traditional practices. Rights and obligations can be discovered by looking at the law and social practices, as well as at the conventions and traditions of particular societies. Most political theorists assume a situation of special rights, where rights and duties are dependent on particular features of individual states and on the historical accident of conventions and traditions.

Another way of looking at the same question is to examine the distinction between reciprocal ethics and pure ethics.[7] Reciprocal ethics arise because of our recognition of our own vulnerability. We can be hurt and we desire not to be hurt. Since other people too are vulnerable, we can hurt them. They also desire not to be hurt. It is therefore in our mutual interest to reach some sort of agreement with potential attackers. We make a reciprocal agreement and the rights which we gain and the obligations which we incur simply arise out of our mutual self-interest and not out of any altruistic feelings about the proper relationship between human beings. The rights and obligations which we agree on also apply only to the people who have participated in making the agreement and not to any group or person outside. Indeed, if we find a group or person who is outside our own group and who looks vulnerable, then there is no reason why we should not attack them if we feel that it is in our interest to do so. Only if we are wrong in our assessment and we find that they can hit back will we propose some agreement with them and bring them within our system of rights and obligations. Reciprocal ethics thus arise out of mutual self-interest and apply to a particular interest group. They are restricted and partial and not really concerned with ethical relationships at all.

Pure ethics, on the other hand, are not partial but universal. They should take account of all of the interests connected with a case and not be concerned with whether a group or person has a special relationship to us or has transactions with us, or whether they are vulnerable to our attack and cannot hit back. Pure ethics would be impartial, favouring neither the group to which we belonged nor any other group or person. Everyone would be treated in the same way unless there were good and relevant reasons for not doing so. Clearly, such a stance is very difficult to achieve because it means a withdrawal of one's own interests, friendships, and emotions. In order to act in an ethical way we must consciously search for the right decision, a decision free from prejudice or partiality. It is a great intellectual achievement.

Of course, actual states embody rules and regulations that serve the interest of their own members. These are examples of the creation of special rights and reflect reciprocal ethics. The law embodies the positive rights and obligations of the members of the state. General rights are really the creation of the ethical mind. They give us a basis for criticizing actual states who are partial in their treatment of their subjects. They cannot be overruled by special rights but they can be ignored. They are concerned with how people ought to be treated and not with how they are actually treated. In that sense they are not rights at all but moral precepts.

A POLITICAL COMMUNITY

We shall develop a very simple model of a political community. The model combines some of the ideas of J.R. Lucas[8] and H.L.A. Hart.[9]

All communities will have members who interact with each other; if their members actually lived isolated lives, then there could be no community. Likewise, members of a community will share some values. The very fact that they are all human beings ensures this. However, they need not share all values, since the community would in that case be a super organism, such as a beehive. Nevertheless, they do need some fundamental values in common. The extent to which they have opposed values determines how much less they are of a community. Political communities exist within a limited territory and do not have untold resources. This means that there will always be disputes about the distribution of resources. The fact that human beings are vulnerable means that they can be hurt and therefore have a desire to be protected. Indeed, if they were not vulnerable, there would be no need for the law and the enforcement of it.

Thomas Hobbes, in the Leviathan, argued that human beings are fundamentally selfish, as their major concern is with self-preservation; conversely, John Locke, in the Two Treatises on Government, argued that they are funda-

A model of a political community

*	Some interaction	
*	Shared values	Basic to all communities
*	Limited resources within a limited geographical area	
*	Human vulnerability	
*	Limited altruism	Basic to all communities (but some theorists argue about whether they are inevitable characteristics of human beings)
*	Fallible judgement	
*	Incomplete information	
*	Decision procedure	A requirement for all communities

mentally altruistic. People are neither entirely selfish nor entirely altruistic. Few exhibit such extreme characteristics. Their attitude often depends on their mood: a beer too much the night before may result in a nasty, selfish reaction to some simple request the next morning. However, people can and often do put themselves out to help others.

In the Republic, Plato argued that, in theory at least, we could have infallible knowledge: a knowledge that was correct and certain, a knowledge of why something was the case and had to be the case, and therefore an insight into necessity. The ability to have this sort of knowledge was confined to a few and it was these few, with infallible knowledge, who should rule. Today we would be more pessimistic and reject Plato's analysis of our understanding. We cannot be certain of our knowledge since it is really no more than opinion and, as Sir Karl Popper argues, even the most certain of our knowledge, science, is tentative and will remain so forever.[10] We are fallible creatures and can and often do make mistakes. Nevertheless, we can be correct in our judgements and therefore are not always wrong. The difficulty for us is that we rarely have all the information at hand to make a completely sound judgement. We therefore have to make guesses. This is one of the reasons why modern governments spend vast amounts of money on collecting data about their subjects' health and environment. Unfortunately, the nature of the collection, its sorting, analysis, and arrangement into meaningful statistics means that by the time that the information is eventually available, in order to help the decision-makers to arrive at the correct decision, it is already out of date and incomplete.

If we look at the model as a whole, we can see that some values are not shared and that therefore there can be arguments over values. The resources are limited and so therefore there are bound to be disputes about their distribution. The very fact that humans are vulnerable makes them touchy and worried about what others do or might do to them. The fact that people are sometimes selfish leads to resentment and sometimes dispute. Our fallible judgement and lack of information point to conflicting proposals and to different interpretations of the evidence. In all, the community will be continually wracked by disputes, which often tend towards violent conflict. Clearly, what is needed is a decision procedure that can make decisions and settle disputes. It is difficult to design such a procedure but far easier to do this than to attempt directly to resolve each dispute individually by the people concerned. The decision procedure would need to be accepted by the parties involved and, in that sense, would be a legitimate procedure.

In our model, the decision procedure would need to reflect the shared values of the community. The extent to which it did not would be shown in tension in the community and pressure to bring the procedure more into line. The model could cope with a Marxist analysis of society as a class society, with the argument that the decision procedure simply was not reflecting the shared values, so that there was pressure to change it. The group controlling the decision procedure would naturally use the media to put over propaganda to indicate that public rather than partial interest was being followed. The argument also takes note of John Rawls' argument that institutions that are recognized as just will lessen tension in society.[11]

The model brings out important characteristics of all communities but what special features would be found in a political community in the Crickian sense of a liberal, democratic community?

CHARACTERISTICS OF A POLITICAL COMMUNITY

We have introduced the notion of citizenship. A citizen will have certain rights as a political person; these rights will set out the degree of the citizen's freedom and status vis-à-vis other citizens. It follows that, if we look at citizenship in an abstract way, the person as a citizen, as a political agent, should be equal to all other citizens. That is, from the point of view of politics, each citizen should be treated equally and have the same rights. We can define the composition of a political community as being made up of citizens, in which we define citizenship in terms of determinate rights which embody the freedom and equality of its members as political agents. The primary task of this association of citizens is to produce rules which will govern conduct and delimit areas of freedom. The law provides the framework which tells us where our freedom lies. Thus political discourse in this restricted sense, because it is concerned with the formulation of the law, must be concerned with the interests of the citizens taken as a whole. It is concerned with the general interest of the community. We therefore have the characteristics of a political community:

1   It is composed of citizens, in which citizenship is defined in terms of determinate rights enshrining the freedom and equality of its members as political agents.
2   Its function is an association for the purpose of producing rules or law which will govern conduct and delimit areas of freedom.
3   Political discourse, since it is concerned with the formulation of law, is concerned with the public interest.[12]

The analysis highlights other features which a political community will have. It will be rule-governed and authoritative, in the sense that rules will be recognized as imperatives that ought to be obeyed. The rules, of course, will also be backed up by power and will need to be enforced and obeyed, applied and interpreted. All of these tasks will be undertaken by recognized public authority. This points to a further feature: if the rules are to achieve acceptance, then the legislature, the enforcement agencies, and the interpretative authorities must be legitimate. The rules need to be enacted by the right people, who are recognized as the correct authority. In that way the rules will be recognized as valid and authoritative, the police as the right people to support the courts in their enforcement of the law, and the judges as the right people to apply and interpret the rules.

The concept of the open society also arises from the analysis thus far. We have seen in our first model that human beings are fallible and have limited information. It follows that people will be putting forward their own opinion for consideration and making their own judgements. They will not be presenting chunks of certain knowledge, and so no opinion or judgement can be considered as completely correct and therefore must be open to criticism and possible change. This point is made clearer when we consider the nature of the political community, because a citizen of such a community has a right to be heard and to have his/her arguments given equal consideration, although not weight, to any other.

The concept of citizenship also gives us an inkling of the ethical base for such a community. Citizenship includes the notion not only of autonomous individuals who are responsible for their own actions but also of respect for other people who are also autonomous individuals and, equally, citizens. It also points to notions such as equality before the law (each should have equal access to the law), equality in the law (the law should not favour any political group), fairness and justice (as a citizen one has the right not to be discriminated against), and distributive justice (the right to be able to live as a citizen, that is, to have a standard of living below which one will not be allowed to fall). It follows, from the general arrangements and relationships within, that a political community should be non-violent. After all, there would be a general acceptance of the rules and a recognition that decisions are made through argument and persuasion rather than by the use of force.

In such a community, citizens would have a duty to obey the law (a legal obligation) and a wider duty to the general values of the community, since it was attempting to establish a particular form of life. There also should not be a conflict between one's duty to obey the legitimate sovereign and his rules, i.e. the rules enacted by the proper process, and one's own conscience. We mean that even if a particular law offended our conscience, we would recognize that it was authoritative and legitimate and that if we disobeyed we could be rightly punished.

We have made a check-list of the detailed characteristics of a political community:

1   Rule governed.
2   Authoritative: laws need to be obeyed, enforced,
    applied, and interpreted; they have their own
    standing rules enacted by the right process.
3   Legitimate.
4   An open society.
5   An ethical base: notions of autonomous, respon-
    sible individuals and of respect for other people.
6   Justice, fairness, and the rule of law: including
    equal access to the law, equality in the law, equity
    (application of the law in a reasonable way), and
    social or distributive justice (a rising minimum
    standard of living for all citizens).
7   Non-violent.
8   A concept of duty to such a community.
9   A relationship of trust between the ruler and the
    ruled.

The final characteristic brings us to a wider consideration of
the relationship between the democratic ruler and the
citizen. John Locke, for instance, develops three criteria of
sovereignty, all of which we can designate democratic.[13]

He starts off with the notion that the sovereign has a
minimum function, which is to protect life and property
from those few people who would rather live off the produce
of others than their own efforts. This is a tightly limited
activity on the part of the sovereign, with the citizens
getting on with their own lives.

Locke's second idea is of popular sovereignty. We
should really control our own lives and therefore make
decisions ourselves. If we enact the laws ourselves, then we
will be obeying ourselves and so will remain as free as
before. However, there is a problem with this argument.
People will not necessarily agree on particular laws, some
will be in favour and some against and therefore there will
be a majority and a minority: why should we, who are in the
minority, obey the law to which we did not agree; in what
way can we remain as free as before?

In grappling with such questions, Locke moves towards
a third solution. Perhaps we should do that which is for the
public good and, as individuals, give up the pursuit of our
own self-interest and be concerned with the good of the

community. This is an idea which borders on paternalism. If we disagree with a particular law, perhaps we can be led to see that it is the most rational thing to do. However, if we are too stupid or immature to recognize the public good, we can perhaps be forced to act as if we could, and in this way be treated as children.

All of these solutions seem to be democratic but one example can demonstrate how they are different. Consider a proposal to ban the open sale of heroin. Under the first theory of the state's limited function and of our right to control our own lives, this could be an inappropriate area for legislation. Under the notion of popular sovereignty, whether or not a law were passed would depend on the popularity of heroin in the community at any particular time. Under the concept of the public good, a law would be passed banning the sale of heroin.

A feature of the three democratic theories is that the law-making institution is legitimate. It is recognized by us as the right authority to make such decisions. Locke considers the basis of this recognition and reaches the conclusion that we have given our consent to its authority: our direct consent. He thus complicates the matter, really unnecessarily, since it is difficult for us to come together and continually give our direct consent to every law and decision made by the sovereign body. Perhaps we can say that we give our tacit consent if we do not protest too much. The notion of tacit consent could justify the rule of a tyrant or a saint; indeed it could be argued that, since we would be less liable to argue with or criticize a tyrant for fear of reprisals, the tyrant would be even more securely entrenched.

Of course, the notion of continually giving our consent is unnecessary. Once we have authorized the sovereign's authority, i.e. recognized its legitimacy, there is no need for us continually to be concerned with every piece of legislation and policy decision. Locke introduces a far more important concept concerning the relationship of the ruler to the ruled, one which seems to have great relevance for modern day politics and the relationship between modern democratic governments and their citizens. The concept is the notion of trust.[14]

Locke argues that the act of trust is the fundamental constitutional act of a political community because it defines the terms of government. It sets out the relationship between the governor and the governed. His argument is that executive right is entrusted to governments only in a conditional way. It is like a legal trust where the authority of the trustee is limited by the terms of the trust. For example, if a trust fund is set up to administer the estate of a child, the trustee is not empowered to use the money for any other purpose, no matter how worthy. If the trustee attempts to act beyond the terms of the trust then he/she has gone beyond the trustee's authority and so can be removed. A government can likewise be removed if it acts beyond the terms of its trust. Locke states:

> For all power given with trust for the attaining of an end, being limited by that end, whenever that end is manifestly neglected, or opposed, the trust must necessarily be forfeited, and the power devolve into the hands of those that gave it, who may place it anew where they shall think best for their safety and security.[15]

We can understand the argument more thoroughly if we look at a normal legal trust. In such a trust we may find three parties: the truster, the trustee, and the beneficiary. In Locke's political trust, however, there is an important modification: the relationship between the trustee and the truster is special because the truster also happens to be the beneficiary. The truster is therefore in an excellent position both to evaluate the continued achievement of the trustee in the exercise of his/her duties and to decide on the degree of discretion to be given to the trustee in the carrying out of those duties. The modification that Locke has introduced is necessary because it prevents his political trust from assuming a paternalistic character, in which case the trustee cannot claim full discretion.

Locke's argument is that executive power is established by trust. Even though it may necessarily possess prerogative power to act for the public good, sometimes beyond the confines of the law, nevertheless it is delimited by trust. If it goes too far in its actions, beyond what we may call the tacit conditions of society - the very general moral and social principles and goals of the community, the trust can be withdrawn.

Locke, moving away from theory, also points out that experience leads us to recognize an apparent paradox, which is that government is entrusted to people whom we do not trust. The paradox can be avoided by placing government under such constraints that politicians will find it extremely difficult to develop their own advantage except in ways that will benefit the citizens. In other words, if fallible men cannot be entirely trusted in politics, institutions must be designed that can be trusted. That is, we need to design constitutions that enable us to get rid of untrustworthy politicians.

The idea is that state politicians have an obligation not to deviate too far from the conventions and traditions of the society that trusts them with power. Of course, in most cases there will not be an historical trust but in a democracy we can assume that there is a tacit trust.

A further insight into the relationship between the ruler and the ruled, in particular that between the individual and the law, can be gained from an argument developed by Immanuel Kant.[16]

Kant makes a distinction between two categories of rule-governed behaviour: the moral and the political. His basic argument is that people can develop and exercise their moral capacity only within a social context. A social context is therefore necessary before people can be moral. It follows from this that, as morality itself depends upon social order, there must be an obligation on the part of individuals, as moral agents, to help to maintain the conditions that allow the possibility of the practice of morality.

Kant's argument, in the sphere of individual morality, is that individual moral agents have a duty to bring about actions that are in accordance with the moral law. They have an obligation, therefore, to bring about a state of affairs which has not yet been realized. However, as citizens or persons in the public domain, they have an obligation to help to maintain the social order: an obligation which is to an existing state of affairs. This obligation is a means to an end rather than an end in itself because it is aimed at maintaining those conditions which are necessary for moral functioning and, of course, they may not be good in themselves.[17]

Taken together, Locke's concept of trust and Kant's argument about the necessity to maintain the social order not only go some way towards providing us with a framework in which to look at the resolution of possible conflicts between private and public morality but also highlight important features of the relationship between a ruler (particularly a democratic ruler) and a citizen.

In taking action in order to preserve the social order

that allows the existence of moral functioning, state politicians are limited by the trust that is placed in them. They have an obligation not to go too far beyond the notions of fairness, justice, and retribution that are contained within the conventions and traditions of the society that they represent. If their acts are too reprehensible, they are, in effect, undermining those traditions. They are going against the way of life of the community and, as its representatives, they are bringing it into disrepute (as Hitler brought Germany into disrepute). They are betraying the trust placed in them by the community and should be thrown out.

An alternative model

Using the checklist on p.71 of the characteristics of a political community, it is easy to see where actual communities might differ from the ideal. For instance:

1   Rule-governed: favouring certain groups.
2   Authoritative: maintained by force and the threat of force, by power.
3   Legitimacy related to force.
4   A closed society: little discussion allowed.
5   An ethical base: self-interest or interest of a group; the use of people to serve the interests of the ruling group.
6   Justice in the interests of the stronger.
7   Violent: decisions made through the use of force.
8   A duty to obey only if one is within the range of the ruler's strike capability.
9   No trust.

The most notable features of such a model are the withdrawal of any real ethical base, and a reliance on power and force.

A Marxist model

A Marxist model would include the following features:

1   Rule-governed: in favour of the ruling class.
2   Authoritative: maintained by force, or the threat of force.
3   Legitimacy: ruling-class control of the means of production; control related to force.

4   A closed society: in the sense that the ruling class, once they come to power, will try to prevent change; however, they will fail to do so because change is inevitable in a class society, owing to internal contradictions.
5   An ethical base: based on the interests of a particular class; ends justify the means.
6   Violent: authority retained by force but as the ruling class diminish their violence increases in order to retain their authority.
7   Justice: class justice.
8   Duty: no obligation on the part of the oppressed, except in the sense of obeying if force is used, but nevertheless a working class duty to the future utopia.
9   No trust.

Notice that in the future utopia the model would revert to something like the political model. There would also be an absolute universal morality, not a relative class morality.

The last two models have been introduced to emphasize the point that reality differs from the political model. This we have accepted but we would argue that our practice does contain elements of the ideal. In our model we have tried to pick out some of the elementary and necessary traits of politics. To present a complete picture is neither the task of this book nor likely to be possible. Nevertheless, we hope that a consideration of these elementary traits of politics will prove of use in understanding the far more complex situation in the real world.

THE JUSTIFICATION FOR A POLITICAL SYSTEM

A number of justifications have been put forward for a liberal society and a political system. The two, as we have argued, go hand in hand, although there could be a political element in a non-liberal society. Probably the most forceful and attractive justification appeared in J.S. Mill's On Liberty. The package of arguments looks very strong but when untied it is very easy to attack each argument systematically.[18] Indeed, the way in which Mill presents his case is a very good example of a political argument, of how to set out mutually supporting arguments which, taken individually, are not very strong. The package contains the following elements:

1   The intrinsic value of freedom: freedom is good in itself.
2   The extrinsic value of freedom: freedom is to be valued because it provides the conditions necessary for other goods, which we value, to come into existence.
3   The liberal society enshrines the idea that we have a duty to respect other persons. This is also Kant's argument, that to coerce a rational being is not to treat the person with the respect required for a true rational being.
4   The political procedures which are set out mostly avoid violence and coercion.
5   Respect for human rights means leaving people free. Mill argues that we should be allowed to undertake any action so long as it harms no one else (a self-regarding action) and that this is a natural right and is self-evident.
6   We are the best judge and guardian of our own interests, and the subsidiary arguments attached to this. No one who will judge our interests less well than ourselves should have the right to do so; therefore we should be left alone in order to attend to our own interests, if by doing so we are not interfering with others attending to their interests.
7   When the state interferes with individuals it often does so for the wrong reasons. It abuses its power.
8   There is no need for the coercive state if the proper liberal/political procedures are followed, that is, if rational beings operate in the demo-cratic/discussion type of society advocated by Mill.
9   If a society is designed in a way that is free, so that all arguments and points of view can be heard, then it is more likely to arrive at the truth than an unfree society where views are suppressed. Notice here that Mill makes the assumptions that a mature, rational person will desire to achieve the truth and that, like an academic community, this is the aim of politics.

Other writers have produced some additional arguments. For instance, Bernard Crick would stress the need for citizen participation in the body politic and the need for political education to achieve this, but Mill really argues this as well. Michael Polanyi, in a pioneering attack on central planning,[19] argues that a political and free society is more efficient, but this is really a form of Mill's argument about the extrinsic value of liberty. Polanyi also includes a biological argument (a vitalist theory of evolution) that a free society is a logical conclusion of the progress of man from the animal.[20] Polanyi, Oakeshott, and Crick also stress the importance of order and the rule of law, and maintain that the free society cannot be disassociated from tradition.

Chapter five

THE NATURE OF POLITICAL ARGUMENT

Before examining the nature of political argument, it may be useful to say something about the nature of the word 'argument' itself. In everyday usage the word tends to be associated with words such as 'disagreement' or even 'quarrel'. 'I had an argument with him' might suggest that some degree of acrimony had occurred between the individuals concerned. This kind of situation comes to mind when considering the phrase 'political argument'.

However, the word 'argument' has another usage, related not to 'quarrel' or 'disagreement' but to 'reason' and 'reasoning'. Thus, we speak of 'valid' and 'invalid reasoning' or 'valid' and 'invalid argument'. A valid argument implies that the correct rules of reasoning have been observed, and that in invalid arguments they have been broken. However, the word 'argument' has an additional connotation. Different kinds of activities tend to observe different modes of reasoning. Thus, the kind of reasoning observed in mathematics is different from that observed in the sciences or in law. Becoming a scientist or a mathematician involves understanding the reasoning forms appropriate to those activities. Most people would be prepared to offer a description of the methods used by the scientist or by the mathematician. They would also be prepared to provide an account of the methods characteristic of these activities. However, the situation becomes radically altered when one is asked to give an account of the kinds of processes that characterize political reasoning. Indeed, cynics might insist that there is nothing within the structure of politics which resembles 'reason' and 'argument' in the sense employed within the physical sciences, mathematics, or the law. 'Argument', when applied to politicians, seems to resemble nothing more than the hurling of insults, resulting in 'arguments' which can be no more significant than 'disagreements'.

DEDUCTIVE AND SCIENTIFIC ARGUMENT

The deductive sciences have attracted the attention of logicians and have had the unique distinction of being ascribed 'valid' or 'invalid'. Deductive arguments give the assurance of certainty. Assertions within mathematics are not 'probably' true but can be demonstrated to be true of necessity.

Deductive reasoning, with its promise of demonstrable certainties, inspired many with the dream of evolving a physical science which could be based on the same incontrovertible certainties as mathematics. This vision of the physical sciences, latent within much of the work of Descartes, was destroyed forever by Hume.[1] He pointed out that the possibility of demonstrable certainty was unattainable within the physical sciences because of the lack of certainty implicit within the empirical premises upon which the demonstration was based. Empirical reasoning could never have the certainty of mathematics, nor could any demonstrably true proposition be applied to the world.

However, the exposure of the fundamental flaw that prevented the certainty of mathematics and logic being reproduced within the physical sciences did nothing to destroy the growing faith in 'scientific method'. Mathematics proceeded by 'deductive' reasoning, physical science by 'inductive' reasoning. Despite the skeleton revealed by Hume, 'inductive' reasoning was as good as 'deductive' reasoning. Recent developments in the philosophy of science have given an alternative account of 'inductive method'. Many would accept Popper's viewpoint that there is no logic of discovery. Some would even throw caveats round Popper's faith in a logic of testing.[2] Yet, however people might differ in their analyses of 'scientific method' or the 'method of reasoning within the sciences', there is a recognizable set of procedures which fulfils the criteria of 'scientific proof'. Science may not be composed of eternal verities but it must at least consist of highly probable, well-supported hypotheses. Scientists know what kind of evidence and what kind of mathematical calculations go into the substantiation of one hypothesis and the abandonment of another.

Additional claims have tended to widen the gap between the methods of the sciences and mathematics on the one hand and activities such as politics on the other. One such is the question of objectivity. There are definite tests for ascertaining the validity or invalidity of proofs within mathematics. Science consists of objective scientific laws, which have their origin in external, observable facts. It is held to be a requirement of science that experiments should be repeatable and that scientific knowledge should be available to all. Assertions in science are about an external reality 'out there'. They are true assertions when they are in correspondence with these external states of reality and false when they fail to be so. On the other hand, analyses of ethical statements have tended to emphasize the subjective nature of these judgements. Statements such as 'murder is wrong' or 'causing pain is immoral' have been interpreted as meaning 'We disapprove of murder' or 'We disapprove of causing pain'. To say something is wrong is merely to express a feeling of displeasure, unease, or taste. In all of this there is the suggestion that it is somewhat quirky on our part that we should find the act of torturing someone distasteful. In one sense, the analysis of ethical statements in terms of individual feeling can be traced to Hume, who insisted that our ethical judgements are founded on feeling and not upon reason.[3] However, the subjectivity of these judgements was mitigated in Hume's case by the belief that certain feelings were common to all people.

There is, of course, no fatal blow to objectivity in the analysis of ethical judgements in terms of feeling, providing that the 'feeling' is not allowed to be the last word on the matter. The feeling of distaste that one experiences on tasting quinine is not the same kind of distaste that one experiences on contemplating murder. This is not a case to be resolved by asking a person to retrospect on their inward state of feeling, i.e. on the experience of tasting quinine and that of contemplating torture. The difference lies in the way in which the participant could be asked to justify their feeling. It makes no sense to ask someone why they experience a feeling of distaste on tasting quinine but it does make sense to ask people why they do or do not experience certain feelings about torture. Hume's insistence that ethical judgements are based on feeling and not upon reason had importance from the basis of ethics. The belief that ethical truths are 'grasped' by reason rested on the assumption that ethical truths are discernible in the way that mathematical truths are grasped. Half-way to Kant's Copernican revolution, Hume placed ethics within the consciousness of human beings. Hume, as is well known, had an extremely tight definition of reason: it is only in mathematics and in the 'observance of relationships' that 'Reason' may be seen to operate at all. However, to remove ethics from the realm of reason or from the realm of Platonic entities does not necessarily relegate the subject to the realm of the irrational and the purely subjective.

In many ways the success of physical science, with a concomitant faith in 'scientific method' and 'inductive' empirical reasoning, has led to a denigration of activities that do not proceed by these methods. The very notion of scientific observation of a definable 'external reality' is designed to replace observations in terms of personal idiosyncrasies of individual percipients by an adherence to quantitative methods. Science is concerned with truths or falsity or at least with the probabilities and likelihoods. Even if we are prepared to admit that the 'objective' methods of the science have frequently been uncritically overdrawn, it would be difficult to deny that the development of scientific method has proved itself to be a highly successful form of reasoning.

However, it would be a pity if the very success of one kind of reasoning concerned with one aspect of human existence should encourage the denigration and abandonment of other forms of reasoning. Thus we might succumb to the temptation to conclude that, when neither experience nor logical deduction can furnish the solution of a problem, we can do nothing but abandon ourselves to irrational forces, to our instincts, to suggestions of violence.

Chronologically at least, the kind of logic and reasoning that we now tend to dismiss as 'inferior' was precisely the kind of logic from which mathematics, symbolic logic, and scientific method could develop so successfully, as Aristotle warned.

The intentions of the politician and the logician, of course, differ. The logician is concerned with the mechanism, the forms of arguments. The politician is concerned with the use of arguments in order to elicit a particular response from an audience. The politician's use of argument is action-orientated. Athens, no less than any other age, had its pedlars and traffickers of illicit arguments. The Athenians, by all accounts, were a particularly litigious set of people. Then, as now, lawyers were concerned not with justice but with obtaining the acquittal of their clients. There are people, we say, 'who would argue that black is white and white black'. There are also people who would 'charm the birds from the trees'. Taken together, these qualities would be a powerful combination.

Athenians taking part in public life needed to have the skills that enabled them to argue about everyday affairs. This was done by means of persuasive language and logical argument, or rhetoric and dialectic. Aristotle observed that 'all men make use, more or less, of both: for to a certain extent all men attempt to discuss statements and to maintain them to defend themselves and attack others'.[4] However, Aristotle obviously thought that too little regard was paid to dialectic. Too much attention was paid to 'prejudice, pity, anger, and similar emotions' and the argument itself seemed of little consequence. Good rhetoric demanded a particular set of standards. It could not be separated from dialect, the art of reasoning rationally, because one of the prerequisites of a persuasive argument (at least Aristotle trusted that this was so) was that it was based on credible premisses and credible influences. Anyone who wishes to become a successful orator 'must be able to argue logically, to understand the people he is addressing and to understand their emotional states of mind'. Dialectic was concerned with argumentation in its widest sense. It was not concerned with a specific type of reasoning that occurred in particular sciences, such as mathematics or medicine. Nevertheless, this generality, this abstraction, did not entitle the orator to ignore the specific conditions of the case, 'whether an argument concerns public affairs or some other subject we must know some, if not all, of the facts of the subject'.

It is the very generality of dialectic reasoning, the kind of reasoning useful for dealing with the rag-bag of everyday affairs, that has been responsible for its low status. Aristotle pointed out that the methodology of particular sciences was different from dialectic. If this was true in Aristotle's day, then it could be held that this applies even more to our own day. Recent notions of scientific method, the great developments in symbolic logic, have changed the situation still more. Nonetheless, it was from dialectic that these logical systems were subsequently developed. Aristotle's insistence on the generality of dialectic lay in his belief that the simple logical laws, which were implicit in the everyday subject matter that was the subject matter of dialect, lay at the heart of all reasoning and argumentation. If these rules were broken then invalidity occurred whatever the subject matter.

Thus, we should not think of mathematics or physical sciences operating with a superior logic and with superior logical principles. We should be incorrect in supposing that it is appropriate to expect a lower standard of logic and reasoning with human affairs than would be exacted elsewhere. It is merely that dialectic remains as a set of logical rules. These, however, cannot be placed into a logical system because, were we to do so, the increased abstraction would render them less employable and less applicable.

We should therefore think of the same logical principles being applied across a continuum of activities with formal logic (unencumbered by the consideration of facts), physical science, law, and politics. The licence of the market place and public arena will allow the persuasive tongue of sales-people and politicians to attempt to conceal basic flaws in their arguments. However, the application of the Law of Contradiction tends to deflate orators who are carried away by their own persuasiveness. Over-enthusiastic politicians, zealous of catching votes and attempting to be all things to all people, might well find themselves committed to promising courses of action that were incompatible with each other and holding views that were contradictory. Skilful politicians may attempt to disguise the insecurity of their position by resorting to rhetoric. Thus, one would expect that politicians would be consistent in their position and that they would not make promises to carry out policies that were incompatible with their claimed position. It was for this reason that Aristotle saw dialectic as a prerequisite of rhetoric. If the pursuit of politics were to be a serious and rational occupation, the persuasiveness of the orator could be effective only when accompanied by sound arguments. Politicians would be expected to observe simple logical rules. These would be that they should not simultaneously affirm their belief in a particular proposition while also claiming a denial of this proposition. Thus, basic rules of logic, such as the Law of Contradiction and the Law of Excluded Middle, can be held to be valid across all forms of reasoning. We cannot, for example, believe both of the following propositions:

1   Apartheid is wrong in all circumstances.
2   There are cases when apartheid is admissable.

However, from these two propositions, we cannot logically deduce any particular form of action. Nevertheless, if we claimed to hold that a particular form of conduct were wrong and then habitually committed those acts of which we alleged that we disapproved, some doubts would be raised about our sincerity. Similarly, we might consider the case of those people who support comprehensive education and then send their own children to public schools.

The success of logic and the construction of logical systems tends to foster a detached attitude towards logical arguments. We tend to think of valid and invalid arguments as enjoying an independent existence, detached from human beings. The fact that computers excel at symbolic logic and play chess tends to endorse this notion of logical systems enjoying an autonomous existence. In a similar way, though not to such a high degree, we think of 'scientific method' confirming or providing evidence for a particular hypothesis as being a mechanistic point of view. However, given that invalid arguments may exist, it is only human beings who are capable of making invalid inferences and who draw wrong conclusions.

The extent to which it is thought appropriate to be emotionally attached to the arguments that one puts forward varies from subject to subject. In the case of mathematics and the physical sciences, it is believed that the arguments speak for themselves. If a good inn requires no sign then one might say that a good, sound argument requires no oratory. Although a mathematician or scientist would regard emotion or oratory to be out of place in a scientific paper, no doubt 'persuasive politics' and persuasive lobbying would be carried on elsewhere. The persuasive use of language would have little purpose because there is a general understanding of the kind of evidence that merits acceptability. On the whole, mathematicians recognize when an acceptable proof has been produced. It is in those areas where evidence can never be conclusive that rhetoric and persuasion are required to fill the gap. As the amount of proof and evidence decreases so the quantity of rhetoric increases.

Most activities owe their success to the fact that the nature and scope of these activities can be defined. The term 'engineering' covers a wide range of activities and techniques. The complexity of these activities has made it necessary to divide the 'engineering' activities into more manageable areas of expertise. As our demand for various technologies increases, the tendency will be to divide these technologies into even more manageable parcels. However, the fact that we call a problem one of 'engineering' defines both the problem and the kind of methods that will be used in solving the problem. The engineer can offer a diagnosis of the problem and can call upon the sciences relevant to that branch of engineering, but the amount of knowledge which is in existence is never in itself sufficient to compel a particular remedy or course of action. Manuals of practice can be produced but 'going by the book' may not suffice, simply because the case in question may have some deviating characteristics, which can be recognized only by the 'art' and experience of the engineer.

Thus, when we consider problems that are concerned with decisions as to 'what should be done' and the best means of accomplishment, there is an inevitable gap between the knowledge, which may be used as a basis for action, and the action itself. An analysis of a particular situation or problem does not contain within it the method requisite for its solution. We do, of course, talk of particular situations 'calling out for reform' and particular conditions 'calling for action now' but what we really mean is that human beings acknowledge that human beings should do something to change a situation which they acknowledge to be unjust. Even when people acknowledge that something should be done at once, they might well disagree concerning the precise action.

The gap between the analysis of a situation and the knowledge basis which may lead to a change in that situation differs according to the nature of the subject matter. In a game of chess, an analysis of the present state of the chess-board and a knowledge of how to manipulate the rules determine the player's next move. This does not exclude the possibility that the player may make a move that is unexpected and totally unprecedented. Being able to manipulate the rules in this way is what we mean by being a skilful player or being a genius at chess. Despite this, however, it would be reasonable to say that the present state of the chess-board, plus the rules of the game, entail the next move that can be made, even though it may require a computer to list what these possible moves might be.

Formal systems of logic have relied on the possibility of

entailments between a certain set of premisses and a particular conclusion. If all finches are grain-eaters and sparrows are finches, it follows that sparrows are grain-eaters. However, the statement of a desired end does not entail the precise method of achieving a particular end. One might go for a walk for the good of one's health or for a dozen other reasons. Equally, one might fulfil the injunction to take exercise for the good of one's health by doing a multiplicity of activities, except walking. We might assume that for the attainment of X, there is more than one way of bringing it about.

Yet, despite the permissiveness that allows several legitimate ends for the attainment of a particular means, our assessment of rationality depends upon the individual's ability to choose a particular means to an end. A person who chooses an inappropriate way of attaining a particular goal would be assumed to be behaving irrationally. On the other hand, a person who hit upon a new method of obtaining a goal might be regarded as particularly innovative and intelligent.

Hume called attention to the logical gap which appeared to exist between the world of fact and the world of values.[5] The problem of how to derive 'an ought from is' is an alternative to the question, 'how can a particular moral judgement be justified by an appeal to "states of affairs"?' The question can be made even wider than it is placed by Hume by asking how any form of action can be justified by an appeal to states of affairs. The problem put in Hume's terms may be insoluble, but we can look at the way in which judgements are made and actions undertaken in a different way.

POLITICAL ARGUMENT

It is chiefly because human beings belong to the species known as 'sapiens' that they have been successful. Humans, as well as having wisdom, are doers and creatures of action. As Kant points out, the world of values coexists with the world of states of affairs. If human understanding of the world is seen as being subsidiary and subservient to the realm of human action, the necessity of describing how an understanding of a situation pushes a person into action seems less important. It may well have been the human preoccupation with ends and the attainment of goals that led Aristotle to suppose that all actions and motions in the universe were for some purpose. The acquisition of knowledge, however desirable it may appear to be as an answer itself, was (and is) primarily sought as a better means of matching up people's expectations and wants with the end that they had in view. Thus, their acknowledgement of suffering and pain led to an interest in healing and medicine, and so science, anatomy, physiology, pharmacology are studied so that this end can be accomplished. The doctor has firstly to diagnose the nature of the illness and then to decide, on the basis of the knowledge of the sciences of medicine, which would be the best form of treatment for a particular patient. Because the science of medicine is an extensive one, not all doctors would necessarily agree about the precise nature of the treatment: doctor X might prefer drug A to drug B. Most doctors, however, who are practising within a particular tradition, would be following precepts, such as 'in situation x, administer drug y or follow treatment t'.

However, there are controversies in medicine concerned not only with methods of bringing about a particular end, i.e. the preservation of life, but also with whether the preservation of life is always a desirable end. The injunction to save life may be in direct contradiction with the alleviating of suffering. Medical science may well be geared to the preservation of life but how is the word 'life' to be interpreted? A human being could be preserved for a long period of time on a life-support machine but in what sense is this human being 'alive'?

It is, of course, the very success of medicine that has led to a fundamental criticism of the Hippocratic ideals. 'Life' must be something more than 'not being dead'. However, the decision to waive or disregard the ideals expressed in the Hippocratic oath would affect profoundly the procedures to be followed earlier in the programme. A set of procedures dedicated to the 'alleviation of suffering' may be different from a set of procedures dedicated to the preservation of life at all costs. One of the important results of a decision to abandon the injunction that the preservation of life must always be a prime objective would be to introduce an additional set of procedures. These would be concerned with the questions of when this should not be the sole objective and what other objectives should be observed instead. These rules and code of practice would be understood and observed by the doctor and would affect the clinical judgement made by the doctor in the treatment of a particular patient. The planning of the treatment of any particular patient would be different, for example, in a situation where euthanasia was an option and where it was not.

Of course, we can see that in the above example the precise pattern to be followed would not always be clear cut and easy to discern. Arguments could occur concerning the desirability of attempting to save the life of a patient, and therefore disagreements might ensue about the nature of the treatment to be given. This kind of disagreement would precede any further disagreement about the practical day-to-day care of the patient, which would arise even when decisions had been made. One might decide not to prolong the life of the patient and therefore, in lay terms, 'make the patient comfortable'.

The above example has the following ingredients: (a) an end, i.e. saving of life, and (b) methods of attaining this end. These methods rely on the judgements of particular medical experts, heavily reliant upon a dependable body of medical science. There is some degree of choice and variability in the way in which making the patient 'comfortable' is carried out. When the end is changed, the treatment, with possible variability, will also change.

If we compare the above argument with the kind of argument that occurs in politics, there will be some similarities and some differences. Politics, like medicine, is devoted to an end but, although there is a possibility of several ends in medicine, the possible ends in politics are much more widespread. The treatment of a patient depends on the professional judgement of medical experts, in the same way that a political solution depends on the 'professional judgement' of the politician.

It is at this juncture that one comes to one of the greatest differences between the kind of reasoning possible in politics and that possible in medicine or engineering. We can speak of the 'professional judgement' of an engineer or a doctor but could there be anything analogous to the 'professional judgement' of the politician? We can dismiss the plea that politicians cannot exercise professional judgement because they are not a profession by asking why we would be unwilling to think of a politician exercising 'professional judgement'. It does not call attention to the difference between 'amateurs' and 'professionals' on the grounds that amateurs are unpaid and professionals paid, since politicians are paid and therefore professional. The reason that there can be no 'professional judgement' rests on the premiss that there is no body of knowledge which allows the possibility of professional judgement. There is no body of political knowledge as there is of 'medical knowledge' or of 'legal knowledge'.

Politics has no subject matter which identifies it as 'political'. On the other hand, it would be equally true to say that everything could comprise the subject matter of politics. Propositions from physics or medicine are discernible as coming from an identifiable body of knowledge. We might consider some of the following:

1 There can be no true equality while parents are permitted to pass on their wealth to their children.
2 Unemployment would decrease if the average working week were reduced to thirty-three hours.
3 Dr X has tested the cabbages for lead content.
4 Say 'no' to a supermarket on Bannister's Field.

The first two statements belong fairly clearly to the kind of subject matter that is traditionally associated with politics. The third statement is less obviously so. However, it may be those very statements which are less clearly political that might throw some light on what we mean by 'political'.

Aristotle considered politics to be a kind of public ethics. This means that the questions 'what is to be done?' and 'how is it to be done?' become also 'according to what principles is this to be done?' The politician must not only consider the prudential question, of how to find an appropriate means to an end, but also ascertain that the purely prudential ends are pursued by ethical principles. While other practitioners carry out their art or science in accordance with axioms or principles that are non-axiomatic, the politician has the hazard of working with principles that are in themselves problematic. The engineer can assess stresses on bridges by means of wind tunnels and computers but the politician has to work with principles that are difficult to pin down.

Politicians must govern, or are anxious to be seen to be governing, in accordance with ethical notions, such as 'the public interest', 'social justice', or 'balancing the freedom of the individual against the good of society'.

The whole of Plato's Republic was given up to an examination of the notion of justice and the just state. To say that 'justice implies treating everyone justly', or 'fairly', is to beg the question. How do we know when a particular law or system of legislation is 'treating people fairly'? Some of the following propositions have been offered as definitions of 'treating people fairly'.

1 Giving the same to everybody.
2 Treating everyone the same.
3 Giving each according to his/her needs.

As Aristotle pointed out, the definitions, if acted upon, would give rise to injustice. Giving the same to everybody would mean that everyone received the same, irrespective of their needs. 'Treating unequals equally', Aristotle thought, could result only in greater inequality. However, a politician who tried to avoid this might run into difficulties. 'Giving the same to everyone' might result in the same level of grant, say, being given to everyone, whether they needed the additional donation or not. An attempt to avoid giving more to those people who already have might be seen to be 'means testing'. Any attempt to implement policies concerned with 'means testing', while it was regarded with disapproval, would be difficult for a politician to take seriously. A politician can act only within a particular context. Only a certain type of argument can be put forward within a particular political setting. A decision to 'give each according to his/her needs' means that those whose needs are small will continue to have small expectations from life.

As politics is the 'art of the possible', most political decisions have to be taken within an economic and political context. Justification for a course of action moves between an appeal to principle and an appeal to facts. Politicians may plan to introduce further charges for Social Security because (a) the total amount of government money spent on Social Security is too large, (b) the way in which welfare benefits are distributed is unfair.

The politicians who assert that the amount of money spent on welfare benefits is too large are making a factual statement. However, when they are asked to explain why it is too large, they may resort to their political principles and values. A government which is in sympathy with the principle of welfare benefits would give a more generous interpretation of 'too much expenditure' than governments unsympathetic to the principle. In the case of the politicians who claimed an unfair distribution, we would expect them to

91

say why it was unfair and to whom. Are the proposed measures the only way of dealing with the alleged unfairness? Does the unfairness arise because some people are receiving benefits who should not be receiving them or because some people who should be receiving them are not receiving them? They could be asked further factual questions about the plight of the people who would be paying increased charges, and about exemptions and the principles on which the exemptions would be made. Politicians will continually be making reference to facts, principles, and values in an attempt to answer questions and to meet criticisms. It might be useful to think of political argument as operating in three stages:

1   An analysis of a particular situation and a general, broad decision that something should be done to change it.
2   A decision is made regarding what is to be done, and according to certain principles.
3   A decision must be taken regarding the administrative machinery that may be necessary for the implementation of 1 and 2.

At each stage, a government will be open to question and the decision disputed.

The government decision to change the present method of local rate collection could be examined in the light of the above analysis. The present rating system has been reviewed and has been found to be defective. Many people may feel that there is something wrong with the present system of rate collection but may be less sure about what is wrong and still more unsure about what could be done to improve the situation. What are the causes for dissatisfaction with the present system? Many people may feel that the burden of rate-paying falls upon too small a proportion of the population. The amount of rate payable is allocated according to the value of the property and not personal income. Many people who do not own property enjoy the advantages of community amenities which are paid for by house-holders alone. The extreme parameter of this kind of unfairness is the case of the widow who stays on in the family home, living on a diminished income. A similar house next door may be occupied by several adults but their contribution to the local rate fund is no more than that of the widow living alone. Levying the rate charge on property would therefore seem to be an unfair method of tax collection, though it might be suggested that a person's residence bears some relationship to the kind of income that they have. However, we might concede that many people would feel that rate levying would be fairer if it were person-based, rather than residence-based. We might obtain consensus so far: that rate-levying should be person-based rather than resident-based. The justification for this would be made on the basis of an appeal to ideals such as fairness and justice. Everyone should pay a 'fair share' towards the amenities which the rates provide. Again, there may be some consensus on this. However, what does 'fair share' mean? Do we mean that it is economically unfair that the widow who lives alone should pay more rates than a family who are earning incomes but who contribute the same as or less than the widow? Or, when we speak of 'unfairness', are we appealing to an 'unfairness in principle'? If the 'unfairness' is based on economic grounds, then measures could be taken to reimburse lone occupants of houses, without engaging in a radical overhaul of the rating system. However, if the objection to the present rating system rests on the assumption that the unfairness arises because many people fail to contribute to the rating system, then the unfairness can be rectified only by making the rate levy person-based. Having established that the rate tax should be person-based, there are still difficulties concerning the precise nature of this person-based tax. Should it be gauged according to the person's ability to pay or the person's consumption of services? As everyone uses local amenities, such as waste disposal, water, and sewerage, to much the same extent, there might be a case for saying that everyone should pay the same community charge. The insistence that, because each person's consumption of community benefits and amenities is roughly the same, the charge for these amenities should be broadly the same is a departure from the principle of 'each according to his/her needs' and the idea that those who can afford to pay should pay for those who are financially disadvantaged.

We might concede that greater fairness would be brought about if the tax were 'person-based'. However, the argument that everyone should pay the same because their consumption of services is the same raises difficulties with the phrase 'the same'. In what sense does the person earning £8,000 per annum and the person earning £30,000 per annum pay the same, if both pay £300 per annum in tax? Although the numerical sum may be the same in both cases, the sum is very different when considered as a proportion of the person's income. In the first case, the rate-payer pays 3.75 per cent of income whereas, in the other case, the cost represents only one per cent. This seems to be an example of 'treating unequals equally, resulting in inequality'.

We might summarize the argument thus far. Taxes which are person-based may appear, prima facie, to be fairer than those which are property-based. However, a tax-levy that is the same across the board may result in treating unequals equally, which could be the justification for the introduction of a tax which, in attempting to eliminate one kind of unfairness, succeeds only in introducing another. The main motive behind the radical change in the rating system is the belief that involvement in the rating system, i.e. contributing to the rates, is a guarantee that the rate-payer's money is more sensibly spent. Is this an appeal to an empirical fact, that rate-payers are more responsible in expending rate-payers' funds, or is it an appeal to a hidden principle, that people who vote in local elections should contribute something to the rate-money that they wish to spend?

The politician's difficulties are not over, however, because there remains the task of introducing an efficient method of collecting the tax. Even the supporters of the general change would lose enthusiasm for the scheme unless a cheap and efficient method could be found to collect the money. How could universal taxation at local level be enforced without the introduction of something like an identity card? There might be fierce opposition to the introduction of such a method on political grounds, i.e. that the introduction of identity cards in peace-time might seem to be the first steps towards a police state. Thus, a political measure which had passed several attacks might fail on the last hurdle of deciding how the changes could be made in practical terms. In an effort to implement an innovation, difficulties of a practical nature may intervene.

In some cases, the end of a programme may be confused with the method, or the method become more important than the initial end. Is socialism seen as a means of improving the lot of working people or is socialism seen as a great goal and a good end in itself? Would a person dedicated to socialist ideals be persuaded that other ways than socialism could be found to improve the lot of working people? If the socialist insists that no other method can accomplish such an end, what is the force of the word 'can'?

Does it mean that no other methods could have the practical effects of socialism and therefore would not be worthy competitors for socialism? (This is an empirical question, even though it is one of complexity and difficulty.) Does it mean that no method but socialism could improve the lot of working people because socialism has intrinsic worth in itself; no other alternative could therefore be considered? The question of whether socialism is an end in itself, or a means to an end, might be determined by examining attitudes towards failure. If socialism were seen as an end in itself, it would be pursued even if it failed to improve the lot of underprivileged people.

Any programme of action which the politician suggests is likely to fall victim to what could be described as the 'law of unforeseen circumstances'. Even a programme of limited intention impinges on a variety of circumstances and situations. A programme which would seem to have limited implication may turn out to have a wider significance. Such a thought led the political traditionalist, Edmund Burke, to espouse inaction, since any innovation could lead to some dire unforeseen consequence.

POLITICAL TRADITION

Political decisions must be understood within a particular political context, within a particular political tradition. What is a political tradition? It does not appear to be a body of information, of rule-like propositions, which is handed down from generation to generation and which each generation learns and then attempts to apply. It is much more a way of going about things which is not directly expressed and is probably not expressible. Michael Oakeshott, when he reflects on the nature of political decision-making,[6] points out that in making a decision we will bring with us a whole array of beliefs, prejudices, and feelings, as well as some prudential and moral maxims which may or may not be applicable. We will also have developed a certain skill in estimating the consequences of actions, as well as certain beliefs about the people and the world around us. To the extent that these beliefs are normative, they will not necessarily be consistent but can point in many different directions and so it will not be possible to satisfy them at the same time. In practice, this means that they cannot be used as a body of norms and principles that can

95

automatically point out to us the right course of action.
Oakeshott calls these beliefs, prejudices, feelings, and
maxims a 'tradition' and he emphasizes that his use of the
word is intended to indicate that a tradition is not made up
of a self-consistent set of ideas. Although relatively stable
these ideas can change. This means that we can learn from
this tradition only by experience, by living in it; it does not
appear before us in the form of formal propositions but
perhaps in the form of practices and institutions.

If this is the case, then the question arises as to how
the political tradition, if it does not lead us to decisions, can
inform us. Practical discourse is the process by which we
find out from the tradition what we should do and how we
should go about justifying our proposed actions. We manage
to pick up from our tradition 'intimations' about the
situation, consequences, and attitudes. These intimations
are aids to reflection rather than pointers in a certain
direction. 'What is sought is a decision which promises the
most acceptable balance in the circumstances between
competing goods' (Oakeshott 1965: 91).

As we have seen, political and deductive arguments are
different. Unlike geometry, we cannot set out beforehand
what may be considered as relevant to an argument because
what is relevant will often depend on the circumstances of
the case. For instance, if we asked a geometrician what was
the colour of an equilateral traingle, we would be regarded
as mad; in politics, however, to ask the colour of the sash
worn by someone's father could be quite relevant. We would
not know unless we knew the circumstances. Political
arguments can often be weak and based on little evidence
but of much value. In geometry such arguments would be
ruled out and would not be considered as any sort of
argument. Political argument, like many practical
arguments, is dialectic in form. The argument goes, 'so and
so, therefore so and so' and then someone else adds, 'but so
and so, therefore so and so'. The key word is 'but'. There is a
logic of one side of the argument and a logic of the other
side of an argument.[7] The right political argument can come
only from the skilled practitioner working in the tradition of
a particular political community.

TEACHING POLITICAL ARGUMENT

The only way to develop techniques of argument is to participate in argument. This is why much time is spent on philosophy courses in presenting an argument orally and engaging in critical debate with one's peers or teacher. Politics is different, in that the arts of persuasion can also be used and that weak arguments often have to be used. Nevertheless, the basic rules of logic must also be followed unless one is going to look a fool.

By participating in organizations such as club management committees, the art of presenting cogent arguments can be developed, as well as other skills and techniques connected with politics. A quite successful way of developing an interest in and understanding of national and international politics, and in particular the method of argument used by the actors involved, has been developed by Nicolas Haines. He calls the approach 'Situational Method'.[8] There are four elements in the approach:

1   A situation which is prominent in the media is chosen, so that much material is available for perusal and discussion. Chosen situations are selected because of their immediate relevance and because there is a likelihood of imminent governmental action within that area.
2   One problem is elicited from the situation; it is expected that other problems which are seen to be associated with it, will emerge later.
3   Principles, which might be expected to emerge in debate while an attempt is made to resolve the problem, are set out and discussed. The discussion aims at finding out the relevance of the principles, whether they can be held consistently and in what circumstances, and the nature of the values on which they are based.
4   An attempt is made to reach a decision based on the arguments used in the public debate, on the group's understanding of them, and on their own additional arguments. This is important, since politics is concerned not only with argument but also with argument aimed at action. Although few discussions in politics are exhaustive, since political argument is open-ended and continues until the participants are satisfied that no more

needs to be said presently, nevertheless decisions often must be made before the debate is ended.

During the ensuing discussion, it should be emphasized that any proposed courses of action must be justified by reference to principles and values, and that these principles and values must themselves be justified in accordance with the hierarchy of values and preferences in the structure of our value systems. Use of this method usually leads to a recognition that politicians in a democratic society must take considerable notice of the customs and traditions of their own society. In a political society it leads to a recognition that compromise is a value of great importance. Compromise can itself be justified by reference to a major principle, namely that the political process must be kept going. In order to be successful, politicians must not only refer to the values and principles favoured by their supporters but also be able to take into account other principles and values without seemingly giving up their own. They must become experts in casuistry.

Principles are concerned with action. They are precepts which advise us what we should do if we desire to bring about or maintain a particular state of affairs. They are therefore derived from values and reflect those values. By values we mean those things (material or abstract) to which people are attached and towards which they have a favourable attitude. They can value something in itself and say that it has intrinsic worth or they can value some item or concept because it leads to other things that they value: it has extrinsic worth.

In using the situational method, the group leader and members should use an interrogatory style. This helps members to formulate points more effectively because of the need to provide justifications for their arguments. It usually results in members heightening their commitment to an answer because they have worked out justificatory arguments in order to support the principles that they have formulated. It also leads them to defend their principles and to look for other supporting principles and values as they engage in battle with their interrogators. After a time, members of the group will no longer put forward a principle arbitrarily because they know that it will be attacked. They begin to see the strengths and weaknesses of different arguments, how arguments can be criticized, and how different principles can come into conflict with each other and must be weighed against each other in reaching a decision. The exercise is really to get members to decide for themselves the strengths of a particular principle; to test their own arguments for consistency and coherence and to attempt to establish a hierarchy of preferences; to find out what value that they put on different justificatory arguments and principles; and, by examining the public debate, to attempt some understanding of the value that society places on certain principles and their justification.

The method also brings out an important facet of questions about principles qua principles: one should refer not to the truth or falsity of principles but only to their reasonableness or non-reasonableness in the particular circumstances, to the reasonableness of the supporting justificatory arguments, and to the results of both following and adopting them. A principle in ethics and social philosophy cannot be absolutely true or barely true but only absolutely reasonable or the most reasonable in the circumstances. We take it into account when making a decision. We give it a weighting.

The situational method is useful in that it puts students into a position where they not only have to understand and analyse the arguments of the participants in the public debate but also have themselves to work within a democratic structure, in which anyone can challenge their arguments and ask for justifications for the acceptance of different principles or proposed courses of action. The fact that the projects are decision oriented, whereby students are asked to consider themselves as decision makers, even when decisions are difficult to make, leads them to recognize a problem of operating in a democratic society. A tremendous effort and commitment to its procedures is needed to make it work. Consensus does not emerge automatically and often arises only because the participants recognize that compromise has great instrumental value in maintaining the system.

THE JUSTIFICATION OF VALUES

One of the difficulties that are met in developing value arguments is the development of justificatory arguments. We propose to consider this from a practical point of view without considering the metaphysical status of moral concepts.

The nature of political argument

A formal justification of moral concepts would require a certain procedure to be adopted. We shall use an adaption of that provided by Paul Taylor in <u>Normative Discourse</u>.[9] Taylor has four stages: verification, validation, vindication, and rational choice. We include a further stage, which we call confirmation, and so have verification, validation, confirmation, vindication, and rational choice.

We verify a proposed action by showing that it is consistent with the standards that we adopt. We validate these standards by showing that they are consistent with higher standards. We confirm them by showing that they are standards within the appropriate value system. We vindicate the value system by showing that it is one of the set of value systems that make up our form of life. A form of life constitutes what we are as a person. We complete the process by showing that we have freely chosen the form of life. We have made a rational choice. In so far as we cannot show that we have made such a choice, our action will be arbitrary but, as Aristotle argues, we can only be as objective as the subject matter allows; thus, if we think about ourselves, what we want for ourselves, and how we should run our lives, perhaps we may then be said to have made some sort of rational choice.

We can look at this process in more detail:

1   Verification   The statement that some action fulfils or fails to fulfil a standard is an empirical statement: it either does or it does not, it is either in accordance with it or not.

2   Validation   Here we are asking whether the standard used is appropriate in the circumstances. One way of demonstrating this is to show that the standard used is derived from a higher standard. This process could continue but, at some stage, we will need to confirm that the higher standard is the appropriate standard.

3   Confirmation   Here we are asking whether the standards used are part of the appropriate value system; or, to put it another way, whether the standards are part of the value system that we think we are using, and whether the system is appropriate for use in the circumstances.

4   Vindication   We are asking if the value system that we are using is appropriate. Does it provide us with the right point of view? We can answer this

only by looking at our form of life, which contains the set of value systems that make up our character, and which reflects our general outlook on life. Ideally, if we knew a person's form of life, we would know which value system would take precedence in a conflict. For instance, a follower of Kant would follow the rule: whenever there is a conflict between moral rules and the rules of long-range self-interest (prudence), do what is moral and not what is prudent. The rule would be derived from the moral nature of the person's general form of life.

5   The final step in the process of justification is an attempt to show that our choice of form of life, the set of value systems from differing points of view, has been made rationally from the possible set of different forms of life. This means that we have freely chosen it and that we have not been pushed into it either by our upbringing or by coercion.

Let us take again the example which we used in Chapter 3, of the old woman whose bag has been snatched, and fit the justification for a moral condemnation into our justificatory scheme.

1   Neutral facts   Old woman walking along street, car stops beside her, her bag is snatched, she is pushed over, thief jumps back into car which speeds away.

2   We give meaning to the neutral facts by applying standards.

3   Verification   We ask whether our belief about the action comes under the appropriate standard, that is, that bags should not be stolen.

4   Validation   We ask whether we are correct in following the principle that bags should not be stolen; we validate the principle by looking to a higher principle, that stealing is wrong.

5   Confirmation   We accept the principle as being correct, since it reflects the framework of values that we have from the moral point of view.

6   Vindication   We ask whether we are correct in looking at the event from the moral point of view and thereby in allowing our moral value system to

take precedence over other points of view. The answer is 'yes' because of our desire to be a certain sort of character, a moral character. Such a character reflects a particular form of life where morality will always take precedence over other values.

7   The form of life that we follow should have been freely chosen. As we desire to emphasize this, we should really call it the ethical form of life rather than the moral. The word 'moral' has connotations of convention and tradition, which indicates that perhaps we have not consciously chosen it, and so our form of life and moral decisions would have an arbitrary element in them.

Chapter six

THE POLITICAL CURRICULUM

We have argued that teaching is concerned with imparting information and skills. The political educator must decide on the sort of knowledge that would be appropriate for political education and the sort of skills that would need to be imparted if a pupil were going to stand a chance of participating successfully in politics. We have also argued that politics is concerned not only about power but also about values, not only about achieving certain value goals but also about achieving them in a way that respects human dignity. It is therefore concerned about the proper relationship between individuals in the pursuit of their political goals.

For the political educator, one way of arriving at a decision is to consider the sort of knowledge that a politically educated person would need to have in order to have any chance of operating successfully within a political context. We are not looking for the knowledge and skills of a prominent politician but for the sort of knowledge and skills that anyone would need to have within an organization in order to stand any chance of success. The person would also need to be committed to Crickian politics (consensus politics) rather than conflict politics, and would sometimes be able to move people in a desired direction. Robert Stradling calls this person a 'politically literate individual'.[1]

Nevertheless, in spite of the reduced requirements for this politically literate person, we can still consider the person to be an ideal type and aim at achieving such knowledge and skills rather than assuming that they are basic requirements. Interestingly, and amazingly if you think about the complexities of organizations, Stradling's proposals are for the 11 to 16-year-old curriculum.[2] However, we shall use Stradling's proposals for such a curriculum as a

checklist for deciding on priorities. He examines the
contents of the political curriculum by dividing it into three
sections: knowledge, skills, and attitudes and procedural
values. He further divides knowledge into propositional
knowledge, and practical knowledge and understanding:
skills into intellectual skills, action skills, and communication skills. The proposed knowledge and skills are to some
extent appropriate to all organizations, not just to the
obviously political, and so they could be included in a course
on social education if political education were thought to be
too controversial. Indeed, a major criticism of Stradling's
approach is that it is too bland, since it ignores not only the
passion and commitment associated with politics but also
the fact that politics is partial and that arguments are
produced in order to forward the interest of certain groups
or parties. Nevertheless, many of Stradling's proposals have
been introduced into a number of curricula for the 11 to 16
age group and beyond.

POLITICAL LITERACY 1

The first question to consider is the sort of knowledge that
we would need to possess if we actually desired to influence
the decisions of a particular organization. We would need
knowledge not only about the organization but also about
how to get things done. The detailed knowledge would vary
from organization to organization and would change over a
period of time. It would also depend on whether we belonged
to the organization or were outside it, and, if we were inside
it, on our position within the institutional hierarchy of the
organization. The first thing that we would need to know, or
recognize and understand, would be our own position in
relation to the person or organization that we desired to
influence. We would also need to know the organization's
formal management structure as well as the informal
structure of authority. For instance, in a club it is often the
Secretary who has the power, rather than the Chairman,
because it is the former who keeps the records, prepares the
minutes, and often writes the agenda. However, it could be
neither the Chairman nor the Secretary but some other
person who has the enthusiasm and drive to get things done.
It could be the case that someone sometimes has the
Chairman's ear, and sometimes not. We therefore need to
know who that person is and when and why their opinions on

certain occasions may be ignored. We thus need to know the usual ways in which decisions are made and any alternatives that are sometimes possible. If we have this information, we are in a better position to consider which approach would be the most successful.

In order to exist, an organization must have resources. An organization's resources include such things as its funding, its building, and the general facilities available to it. As an aspiring politician, we would need to know what these resources are. We would also need to know alternative or possible sources of funding and the availability of alternative facilities. We would need to know whether a change in, say, the image or the constitution of our organization could make untapped resources available. The available resources must be distributed within the organization, so we would need to know on what basis (need, equality, cost effectiveness, etc.) that the distribution would be made, possible alternatives, and the arguments in support of them. We need to have not only factual information but also an understanding of disputes that have arisen or are likely to arise, of political issues that may be relevant to political decision-making, of the arguments that may be used in disputes or with reference to particular issues. However, as politics is also about moving people in the direction that we require, we also need to know the policies that people actually promote and their political outlook, including the values which they hold and the goals for which they aim. Stradling classes this sort of knowledge as 'propositional knowledge'. His other 'sub-knowledge class' he calls 'practical knowledge and understanding', which is a practical knowledge of the actual issues in dispute and of the people and groups who promote certain policies and goals. He includes in this class an understanding of the nature of disputes and their causes, and of how they may affect oneself, one's group and any other groups; really a practical understanding of how the decision-making process works and of how one can influence it. He points out that the process may work in different ways, depending on the context, and that channels of influence may be appropriate in some circumstances but not in others. The politically literate should also have an understanding of basic political concepts, such as conflict, decision-making, rules, consent/dissent, and knowledge of where to obtain the information that they lack (i.e. whom to approach, which organization to contact, where factual information might be located).

With regard to skills, the politically literate person would require, under intellectual skills, the ability to interpret and evaluate political data; to sort out and organize the data according to political concepts and generalizations; to decide what material is appropriate and what is not; to apply reasoning skills to political problems; to develop the appropriate arguments by such skills, together with the factual evidence; to recognize the possible consequences of taking or not taking certain actions in different contexts. Taken together, we can say that these are the skills that are necessary in order to make the appropriate political judgement in the right way, at the right time, and in the right place.

Under action skills Stradling includes the ability to participate in group decision-making, and the ability effectively to influence and/or change political institutions. We could also include under this heading the ability to make decisions because often, even in democratic organizations, many decisions have to be made very quickly, after inadequate discussion and with minimal information. The skills of the executive are necessary in all organizations. Ideally, in democratic organizations, everyone should develop such skills.

Under communication skills Stradling suggests the ability to express one's own interests, beliefs, and viewpoints through the appropriate medium. We could also include the ability to do the same for a group that one may represent or support: the ability to participate in political discussion and debate; the ability to recognize and understand the interests and beliefs of others; the ability to exercise empathy, i.e. to develop the technique of understanding from the other person's point of view. More significantly, because politics is about moving people in the direction that one desires, one needs to develop the art of persuasion: the ability to put together a convincing and eloquent speech, to manipulate the emotions of the audience. After all, in politics weak arguments are better than no arguments, and so a political practitioner needs to be able to put over ideas in the best possible form.

Stradling includes in his final section, 'Attitudes and Procedural Values', a willingness to adopt a critical stance towards political information. To this we should add 'argument' because, as we have seen, political arguments will often include rhetorical devices which are designed to persuade the listener. A degree of scepticism about political arguments, evidence, and political consequences is a desirable trait in a political practitioner.

Stradling suggests that we should include a willingness to give reasons for our holding a particular view and that we should also expect other people to give reasons in support of their own position. This is really an essential component of political discourse and reflects the political ideal of doing things for good reasons, underlining that political actions are justifiable and not based merely on force. Of course, we could include as a good reason self-interest or group-interest. However, it is hoped that the discourse of the experienced political practitioner would at least bring out these legitimate interests into the open rather than allow them to remain hidden behind platitudes about the public interest.

To argue that potential politicians should show a respect for evidence in forming and holding political opinions seems obvious but it does suggest a limitation on the skill of making the best use of the evidence available. It indicates that arguments should at least have some factual base and should not be complete flights of fantasy. The previous comments about the need for a sceptical approach to evidence and arguments should always be kept in mind by the listener. However, we also need to bear in mind that in politics, as in most subjects, the evidence is rarely cut and dried. It is normally incomplete, and our understanding of it depends upon our interpretation of it and our point of view.

Stradling also argues that one should be willing to be open to the possibility of changing one's mind in light of the evidence. He actually states 'one's own attitudes and values', which seems even more problematic. One should indeed cultivate the ability to weigh evidence and assess arguments, and to examine the possible consequences in the light of the proposal and the resulting action. One should also recognize the nature of political evidence and arguments, and recognize that, as human beings, we are fallible. This would suggest that, on grounds of rationality, one should be prepared to change one's position and that it may indeed be politically expedient to do so. However, the argument surely cannot apply to the fundamental attitudes and values of the political approach which, as we have argued, is part of a particular form of life and is something to which we need to be committed. For instance, although evidence suggests that politics is about force and that people are devious and follow self-interest, does that mean that we should give up an ethical stance? Or (the perennial dilemma of politics), should we be prepared to give up the game of politics and to resort to force if the evidence indicates that, in dealing with certain developments in our society, the political approach is not going to succeed and could in fact lead to the collapse of our political system?

Stradling concludes his list by looking at three fundamental values which are inherent in a political community: fairness, freedom of choice, and toleration. Fairness, he argues, should be used as a criterion for judging and making decisions. We agree with this but whether or not fairness should be the sole criterion or one of a number of criteria depends on one's position in the political game. Could it not be argued, for instance, that if one represented a particular pressure group then the interests of that pressure group would come first, even if the consequences of following that interest successfully would be detrimental to other groups within the community? However, if one happened to be the sovereign (or legislator?) then ideally one should be concerned with questions of fairness and justice.

The question is concerned with the ideal and with practice. In practice, politics is about the clash of interest groups, whereas the ideal is about creating harmony, following the public interest, following fairness and justice. From one point of view, it is a distinction between the universal aspect of politics (politics as a moral realization) and the executive aspect of politics (politics as a method of getting things done). In practice, we attempt to develop, through the law and conventions, a framework for practical politics, and we try to design political institutions that will put into effect the universal aspect of politics, i.e. that will be concerned with developing impartial, universal laws which serve the public interest. In dealing with this aspect of politics, we can see the temptation to develop a theory like Plato's, where he develops the idea of the guardians who have infallible knowledge and an insight into the good, or a theory like Rousseau's General Will, which need not be the majority will and is likewise infallible. In practice, we have to develop man-made institutions, which are occupied by rude and ignorant politicians who have the awesome task of reflecting the universal in their deliberations and legislation.

Stradling points out that the sort of attitudes, knowledge, and skills that he writes about for the politically literate are those which are required within all political contexts, whether it be the state, workplace, union, college, school, etc. Many of the requirements for political literacy may be developed by participation not in party politics but in these other organizations, since all organizations have a political element within them. Quite clearly, therefore, much of the knowledge and skills associated with politics could be introduced less controversially under such headings as interpersonal skills, organizational knowledge and skills, communication skills, public speaking, rhetoric, or logic.

We have already pointed out that we believe that Stradling is too bland in his analysis of politics and that it needs to be brought a little closer to reality. Betrand de Jouvenel argues, for instance, that it is profoundly unsafe to assume that people act rationally in politics, that violence is often the norm in politics, and that peaceful politics in Britain is something that only came about in the eighteenth century.[3] Defeated politicians need no longer fear the loss of their land or their head. He also draws our attention to the fact that manners in politics is an important feature of British politics. 'The game of politics in its Parliamentary guise obtained a good reputation, thanks to its manners in nineteenth century England,' but this was because 'neither the players nor third parties stood to lose from the game.'[4] However, if vital interests change and begin to clash, the game itself is at risk. De Jouvenel is suggesting that politics may be merely the appropriate mode of procedure for a certain time in history.

It can be seen that Stradling, like many other liberal writers, tends to associate politics too closely with the pursuit of the truth as exhibited in the academic community, where decisions are made by people who attempt to be impersonal and impartial. They do things with a universal intent. However, this is rarely the case in political decision-making because decisions are seldom taken by neutrals or by the impartial observer. Commitment to a line is a feature of politics.

POLITICAL LITERACY 2

In a workshop on political education, run for teachers who were interested in the introduction and development of political education, the group came up with the following list of answers to the question, 'What should we do in political education? Interestingly, only one person out of ten pointed out that the suggestions must refer to a consensus, liberal model of politics and political change rather than a conflict model of politics and change.

The curriculum

1   An ethical base should be developed, which would include respect for others, tolerance, and an understanding of the principle of treating others as one would like to be treated oneself.

2   A consideration of how rules can be changed, and generally of how to get things done. Under this heading, the group looked at the following.

(a)   The nature of rational argument: deductive and inductive argument, the dialectical form of political argument.

(b)   Persuasive argument: the use of emotive terms, persuasive definitions, making the best use of evidence, the presentation of arguments and evidence, logical fallacies, and rhetoric.

(c)   Pressure: the use of threats, bargaining, argument on merits, the formation of interest groups, hierarchical pressures (how to use a hierarchy within an organization in order to put pressure on certain members of that organization).

(d)   General political skills: organization of campaigns, how to get support, how to exercise and develop influence, the need to develop an understanding of the function and conduct of meetings.

(e)   Communication skills: presenting oral and written arguments, public speaking, the art of debating, persuasive techniques.

3   Nature of rules and authority.

(a)   Necessity for rules.

(b)   Connection of rules to power and authority.

(c)   Notion of legitimate rules and authority, de facto and de jure authority.

(d)   Different types of rules, e.g. H.L.A. Hart's primary and secondary rules.[5]

(e)   How to get rules changed.

4   Concept of obligation to legitimate authority.

(a)   Relationship of morality and the law.

(b) Individual conscience and the concept of sovereign authority.
5 An understanding of some basic political concepts, e.g. freedom, equality, justice, the rule of law, and of some of the arguments related to these concepts.
6 An understanding of the basic structure of central and local government.
7 Some understanding of the working of the national and international economy.
8 Some knowledge of recent British and international history.
9 Self-analysis.

There was much discussion about the nature of the ethical base, the idea of self-analysis, and the very concept of the political community and political education. In particular, they considered the suggestion that politics was an attempt to lift power relations out of the concentration on force and reflected a special way of looking at the world, a form of life, which could be seen by an examination of its ethical component.

The ethical base

1 Self-analysis A need to examine one's motives for proposing or undertaking an action, since only in this way is it possible to realize whether or not one is undertaking an action for moral or other reasons. One would need to take into account such factors as self-interest, emotions, social influences, conventional and religious influences, and morality.
   A moral act is to act as a rational being for the sake of morality; to take into account all of the interests involved in the decision and not to be partial in the decision, to act as an impartial observer, to act as if one is a moral legislator.
2 A recognition that other people are like oneself, that is, they have the capacity to be rational and potentially moral beings. Such a recognition leads to: a respect for others; tolerance, as one surely must recognize the difficulty of obtaining such a moral status; an acknowledgement that others should be treated in the same way as one would like to be treated; an appreciation of other people's interests and

111

that their interests should be taken into account; an awareness that other people are at least as likely as oneself to achieve moral goodness.

3   A recognition that morality, although it may refer to the mores of one's own society and therefore be based on convention, is intersubjective. The ethical principle is universal and applies to everyone. Take, for example, the Kantian principle, 'Act only on that maxim which you can at the same time will to be a universal law.' The action can only be considered to be ethically right if, and only if, one can consistently will that the maxim or rule involved be acted on by everyone in similar circumstances.

In the self-analysis section of our ethical base, it is a requirement of an ethical act that it be freely chosen and that it is rational. If this is to be the case, then in making an ethical decision we would need to analyse our own motives in order to find out whether the action was actually being undertaken for an ethical reason or whether such a reason was non-existent or subordinate to another motive. Quite clearly, in undertaking such an act, we would be undertaking a particular act: an ethical action, but what is an ethical act? We argue that it is an act which consciously takes into account the interests of other people. Persons acting ethically should not be solely concerned with their own interests or the interests of their group but with the interests of everyone involved in the proposed action. We can see that we can make this formulation of an ethical act into Kantian morality by taking up the view of the impartial observer and by following the categorical imperative: 'Act only on the maxim which you at the same time will to be a universal law'. However, this maxim seems to be a maxim that only God may follow and not mere man and is the reason why, of course, it is a categorical imperative to man and not to God. The way in which we have formulated it, following Peter Singer,[6] recognizes our own interests and takes them into account. We are really taking up the standpoint of an interested participant who consciously tries to be fair and impartial.

The model developed in the workshop was probably too Kantian. However, it did bring out the essential features of an ethical stance: that it is a conscious attempt to develop an approach to human relationships, which is fair in the sense that it does not attempt to do somebody down for irrelevant reasons; that it is not partial, in the sense that it takes into account everyone's interests and not just those of the decision-makers or their groups; that it is rational, in the sense that the decision-makers withdraw their emotions from their analysis and consciously try to work out the interests involved.

We are not arguing that it is irrational to act immorally or amorally. For instance, if we decided to act for the sake of self-interest then it could be a free and rational choice and we could well choose the necessary means to bring about the desired end. David Hume argued that the choice of a goal is irrational whereas the means may be rationally chosen. We are arguing that we can rationally choose to take a particular point of view and rationally apply the standard appropriate to that view. This is clearly the case with ethics. To act in an ethical way may well be opposed to our basic instincts, as it may put ourselves or our group at risk. It is a course of action that we have chosen because we believe that certain values are important to us as a person and as a human being. As we have argued before, an ethical stance is an intellectual achievement and has been developed by us because of our respect for others as human beings, our respect for the human condition. This is what Kant really meant when he stated that we should act for the sake of duty to the moral law; the whole notion is part of a particular form of life.

Much of modern meta-ethics is misguided because ethics is based not on emotions (morality maybe) but on a rational decision to attempt to be impartial. In following morality we may well be following the conventions, the mores of our group, or our own prejudices but in acting ethically we have consciously chosen to act in accordance with a particular form of life and from a particular point of view that we have chosen. We have chosen it because it contains a particular view of humanity which gives man dignity.

A PROBLEM OF ETHICS

Two obvious problems arise when we consider education and the nature of politics. A feature of politics is that it is often concerned with putting forward one side of a case, with arguing and producing evidence for a particular line. In that sense it cannot be impartial. Politics also has its darker side where half truths, downright lies, and threats, and force are used. How can real politics fit into the ethical stance that we have argued is at the base of politics? We can, of course, use the obvious philosophical manoeuvre and argue that ethics and our brand of politics is about 'ought', whereas the dirty politics of the market place is about 'is'. If the 'ought' and the 'is' are too far from each other, however, can there really be any relationship between the two or do we have to accept that politics is solely concerned with the exercise of power?

We can consider politics at three levels: in the market place, in executive decision-making, in legislation.[7] In the market place, everyone argues for their own interests; at the executive level, an attempt is made to reconcile these interests and to make decisions under the loose heading of the perceived public interest; at the legislative level, a conscious attempt is made to universalize certain decisions by exacting law that is not partial but is applicable to everyone. Indeed, it is generally accepted that law that is partial and that does down certain groups is bad law. The judiciary is at the same level as the legislature because it is there to interpret and apply the law impartially. The legislature also has the very practical function of keeping a check on the excesses of the executive. Of course, if this procedure is going to work successfully, there must be a general recognition that it is a fair procedure and the right procedure. In that sense the executive is bound between the parameters of the community's traditions and perceptions of shared values. If it is not, then it must rely on force. The argument indicates that a political community has at least a conventional moral element within it and that we can make room for partiality at certain levels of the procedure. The theory also strives for a pure, ethical component but it is already related to the practice because, within the practice, there is a moral element which in theory can be refined by an ethical critique aimed at universalization. Thus, our brand of politics, although it is about 'ought', does have a relationship with practice and can be used as a running critique with a desire to serve the public interest.

As we have indicated, we can and must make room for partiality within politics. Politics is a pursuit for real people with real desires and interests. The public interest cannot be something that is divorced from these desires and interests. It is therefore quite legitimate to develop the strongest arguments to further our own interests and those of our group. The methods which we use to further our interests will be controlled by the conventions and traditions of the community, and clearly we may occasionally overstep the mark. A part of political expertise lies in knowing how far we can go in the pursuit of our ends. However, from the moral point of view, if we can do right, we can also do wrong. It is part of our education to learn the distinction.

We have argued that it is quite legitimate to develop the strongest arguments for pursuing our interests. Because of this, it is essential that a political participant learns the necessary skills associated with the weighing of evidence and the assessment of arguments.

PRACTICAL POLITICAL ACTIVITY

Much of the argument in this chapter has been concerned with looking at the possible contents of political education. Although we have written about communication skills, the understanding of organizations, the art of persuasion, and so on, much of the approach has remained theoretical. In this section we want to suggest a more practical approach to political education: doing politics rather than talking about politics. Following Professor Ridley's argument, that political education should be an education in how to get things done, we shall give some examples of the sort of knowledge that we would need to have if we were going to operate successfully in the political arena, and suggest that we could develop resource centres for advice and ideas about how people could participate in political activity. The field, of course, is vast. The point is that political education does not end with schooling but is a continuous process which can be carried on in youth clubs, football clubs, pressure groups, as well as in more recognizable political activity in local government. John Stuart Mill argued that we cannot expect to work a political system, let alone perfect it, unless we are prepared to participate and gain experience from working it.

We approach practical activity in two ways, firstly from the point of view of the individual and then briefly from the point of view of the group.

An individual

An obvious case for political education is when an individual has a grievance which he/she wishes to redress against a state institution. As an example, we shall assume that an

115

individual has a grievance in the area of social security, and we will examine some of the pitfalls and considerations that should be taken into account.[8]

If we, as individuals, are blocked by an official, the obvious move is to try to go above the official's head to a superior. The idea is to see a person of higher status, a more senior officer who will be able to review the activity of the official who has blocked us and who perhaps will decide in our favour. Following the guidelines that have been suggested, we should not only look at the situation from our own point of view but also attempt to do so from the point of view of the superior official. We should attempt to empathise with the official.

A dilemma for the superior official is that, if he reverses the decision of the lower official, he will be unpopular. He will be giving the impression not only that the subordinate is incompetent but also that subordinates in general are not up to their jobs and that he himself is reluctant to delegate responsibility. Such an action could also have an adverse effect on morale and on the superior's own position as a manager. On the other hand, as a public official, he should be concerned with the complaint and so he is almost bound to take some action.

It can be seen that the situation could also hold some risk for the individual who has complained. The senior official could be led to add his own weight to the decision of the lower official so that the complainant would have to withdraw or else attempt to go even higher up the hierarchy.

An associated problem in dealing with officials is their own self-image of autonomous officials who are recognized as professional persons, who have the authority and competence to make decisions, and who rarely make mistakes. In practice, few professionals or senior professionals achieve this status but, in an extreme example, a professional may have achieved such authority that a challenge to that authority will be considered by a quasi-judicial body. General practitioners have apparently achieved such status and authority, so that a challenge to their expertise is so shocking that it must receive special treatment. Members of many other professions and semi-professions crave such recognition and therefore very much resent attempts to go above their head. However, in many cases, the situation is complicated by the fact that an informal recognition of autonomy may have developed between superior and subordinate. Thus, head teachers will rarely reverse the decision of a teacher; professors recognize the autonomy and (currently) tenure of the lecturer. Such informal recognition sets up a special relationship between the superior and the subordinate, whereby the reversal of a decision could almost be seen as an unprofessional act on the part of the superior.

We can see that a number of factors need to be taken into account by the aspiring complainant.

1   The formal professional relationships between officials.
2   The informal professional relationships.
3   The desire to remain on good terms with professional colleagues.
4   The desire to maintain morale amongst staff.
5   Mutual blackmail: 'If I put down my inferior, he might tell my boss about my areas of incompetence.'
6   Can the inferior official be replaced if he takes umbrage and leaves?
7   Trade Union pressure: 'Will I get a visit from the local shop steward or secretary if I upset the inferior official?'
8   Bloody-mindedness: a dislike of people who complain; an increased dislike when a person continually complains; a positive determination to inconvenience people who regularly complain.

Clearly, from a political point of view, it is very important to get to know our opponents, their likely reactions, and the side-effects of their activities and our own.

If we continue to be blocked in our grievance and we still think that we have a case, then the obvious people to contact are MPs and councillors. The vast majority of MPs run surgeries in different parts of their constituencies which individual citizens are able to attend, and it is always possible to write to MPs in the knowledge that they are likely to respond because we are voters. Complaints are usually of two kinds: those about services that are run by state institutions, which are the direct responsibility of Parliament; those about local services, which are the responsibility of the local authorities. In theory, MPs could be expected to deal with the former but not the latter but, in practice, since many people do not understand the distinction and blame the central government for all mismanagement, MPs tend to pass on the complaints to the local authorities.

Occasionally, MPs use question time in the House of Commons to publicize specific problems that are of general interest. This leads to civil servants spending much time in preparing the answer to questions. An MP's interest will often encourage senior management to become interested in a grievance in order to demonstrate the competence and fairness of their department.

In local government, as local services are the responsibility of committees, every member of a council will sit on at least one committee and will thereby take part in the operation of some council activities. Those in the chair at committees become closely involved with senior officials in the decision-making of the services for which the committees are responsible. Since councillors are so closely involved in the activities of the council, it would appear that they should be ideal as representatives of local interests and that they should also be better at articulating the case of and giving support to aggrieved individuals. Conversely, it could be argued that their closeness to the decision-makers could inhibit their advocacy of individual grievances. Nevertheless, councillors do seem to be a useful way of obtaining a response to complaints about local services (with the proviso, however, that if they themselves feel partly responsible for the relevant decision, the response may not be wholehearted). From an individual's point of view, it is clearly a good idea to get to know councillors and their interests and influence. A personal approach to individual councillors may well achieve a better response than a general complaint to the council.

In some areas of state authority, such as state security benefits, there is also the possibility of appeals to administrative tribunals. Appeals to the courts and, of course, to legal aid centres, may be made. Citizens Advice Centres can also be helpful.

In recent years, some people have seen the welfare rights movement as a vehicle for political education. It has developed as a reaction against paternalism and deference. Left-wing writers have argued that any political gains on the part of the working class have come about not because of the altruism of the ruling class but because of a fear of the consequences of not meeting the former's demands. The welfare rights movement probably originally grew out of the experience of direct political action in the Campaign for

Nuclear Disarmament, but also out of a growing awareness of the conditions of the poor and unemployed which was brought about by improved social statistics. Welfare rights is also in the field of interest of the new professionals (the social workers) and intellectuals who arose alongside the rapid development of the universities and polytechnics in the 1960s.

Members of the welfare rights movement had to recognize that the underprivileged are often apathetic and ignorant and that they have to be stirred to action. The intellectuals had to be prepared to proselytize and organize. Political action itself has an educational function as people learn to understand and operate the system. In left-wing circles, a frequent question for debate is the extent to which the intellectual should lead or should advise and activate. This is a question with which Lenin tried to grapple in his What is to be done?[9]

Group activity

We have seen that representative democracy has come under fire in recent years for a number of reasons: the tenuous link between the electorate and politicians; the oligarchs within political parties; the weakness of Parliament in relation to the executive; such weakness of opposition parties as compared to the Government that it has been argued that real opposition must come from within the ruling party and from a revitalized House of Lords.

For those who wish to increase the extent of self-government, two possibilities seem to exist: an attempt to remedy the weakness of the system of representative government or an attempt to find new ways of achieving control over the activities of government. However, proposals to increase direct control of involvement in government or administration tends to imply new approaches to representation.

Participation has become the by-word and is, for many people, what political education is all about: if we can encourage people to participate then all will be well, as they will think that they are part of the system. However, participation and involvement can simply become catch-phrases, rather than a real solution to the problem of an ailing democracy (ailing, that is, to the parties not in power). We fear that many people do not share in making decisions and even do not care that such a gap has grown up between those being governed and those governing. It also seems obvious that, without an effective shift of power, participation will be a sham and could lead to an even greater disillusionment with the system.

Many of these complaints come from people who do not have the patience to act politically, to gain the knowledge and learn the skills. There are many ways to participate, as the militants of the left showed so successfully in their virtual take-over of the Labour Party in the seventies. For instance, it is very easy to join a local branch of a political party and, by assiduous canvassing, to gain an influence in that branch. Even committee members are often apathetic and reluctant to take on the responsibility of becoming an officer of a branch. Many branches choose the party candidates for the local council elections and, in some localities, this is virtually the same as choosing the local councillor. In many areas, because of the low percentage of people who bother to vote in local elections, it is also not too difficult to put up alternative candidates and then to drum up enough support to have them elected, even against the party organizations. Anyone can be an election agent and most people can be a candidate.

Of course, people are much keener to participate when an action or non-action threatens them. A check can be kept on planning proposals in local areas and objections may be lodged to proposed plans. Groups can be formed very quickly and letters may be distributed to those likely to be affected, setting out the arguments which letters of protest might indicate.

There are many pressure groups which people can join, although by their nature they represent minority interests. Nevertheless, it does appear that politicians and administrators are much more likely to be influenced by pressure groups than by the actions of separate individuals. Groups open up the public debate and give officials someone to talk to. This makes the latter generally aware of public feelings. There have been a number of successes for groups who are concerned with their immediate environment, perhaps the most notable being the opposition to the development of a third London airport at Stansted. There have also been successes for groups attempting to prevent the dumping of nuclear waste in their area. On a wider scale, there has been the notable success of the Greenpeace Movement in getting people at least to recognize ecological dangers.

Most pressure groups against public or private development gain their members from the middle class. This is often a great advantage, as it enables professional expertise to be used and social/political contacts with top administrators and politicians to be made. Nevertheless, it can have its drawbacks. Thus, for instance, in the case of Stansted, there was a good deal of support for the development of the airport among the local populance, as it would have greatly improved job opportunities and options and probably raised the general level of working-class wages in the area. The support for the proposals was not properly vociferated, however, as it was overwhelmed by middle-class control of the media and by the combined forces of the local landowners and commuters.

A manoeuvre that is often used by officialdom in many planning disputes is to state that the opposition is concerned with self-interest, whereas they are concerned with the public interest. As we have pointed out, being concerned with self-interest is, in reality, a respectable occupation in a democracy.

Many of these pressure groups cause great ire in local communities and so it may be unwise for a teacher or a youth leader to suggest, or even to organize, the involvement of their groups in any such activity. However, the ecology movement does provide some useful opportunities. It is increasingly non-partisan and is concerned with improving the environment. It is particularly open to enthusiastic young people who have the energy to move around the countryside and collect evidence.

Whereas pressure groups are very often concerned with opposition to proposals, community action or direct action is concerned with getting things done. It is much harder to get things done than to prevent things from happening and thereby preserve the status quo. Action often involves a re-allocation of resources and is therefore likely to meet much opposition. There are two major strategies open to such action groups, one of which, if followed, could lead to clashes with the law. The first is a bargaining strategy whereby pressure is exerted on the authorities by argument and evidence. Working-class groups often lack the resources and contacts to formulate their case, and that is one of the reasons why Professor Ridley suggests that the role of the political educator should be as adviser and resource centre, giving actual advice on arguments, the collection of evidence, contacts, and alternative tactics. The second strategy, which is an extension of the bargaining strategy, is a confrontation strategy. It is used when authorities are unwilling to accede to good argument and evidence. A confrontation strategy is often used by trade unions, who threaten work to rule or withdrawal of labour, but a form of it may be practised by direct action groups, organising demonstrations, squattings, sit-ins, rent strikes, etc. The arguments against such action are that there are proper channels through which pressure groups may state their views, and that these activities go against the rule of law, thereby offending political and democratic practice. However, there is a certain flexibility within a political system and it may sometimes be possible to widen the boundaries of acceptability. The publicity gained by such actions is doubtful. It may embarrass the authorities, so that they offer a compromise, or it may bring the pressure group itself into disrepute.

Another possibility for group action is that which provides a service for disadvantaged sections of the community and which is not being provided or is inadequately provided by public or private agencies. Action such as helping old people with their gardens or providing social visits does not put pressure on the authorities to provide such services, nor does it oppose any proposal, but it does provide an opportunity to participate and enables groups to find and recognize resources and to develop contacts.

Chapter seven

IMPARTIALITY, BIAS, AND CONTROVERSIAL ISSUES

We have seen that politics is inevitably wrapped up in the educational process because politics, in the wider sense, provides the values and the goals that are important for our society. This does not mean that it must provide an ultimate goal for our society, a sort of Platonic Utopia; after all, a Utopia for us might be a hell for a future generation. We have indicated that, from an epistemological point of view, we cannot be sure that our view of social justice need be a view that can last for all time. However, politics does include within its own definition certain concepts about procedures and our relationship with others. It is these procedures and values related to human conduct that we need to include in our educational curriculum.

We have argued that the element that differentiates politics from other power relationships is the ethical. It is this dimension that is essential in the development of education. The principle is clearly demonstrated in the concept of citizenship, where citizens are seen to have equal rights and duties and are assumed to be responsible people who are able to make rational choices. In that sense we would say that they are autonomous. The notion of autonomy, or of the autonomous human being, reflects the concept of the ideal human being (a God or an angel) and allows us to make a distinction between animals and <u>homo sapiens</u>. As a species, human beings only have the potential to act autonomously. In theological terms we could say that they share in the reason that is God's. The argument is produced in this way in order to prevent arguments such as those that point out that some humans are not rational and some animals are more rational than some human beings. Our argument is that human beings as a species have a potential capacity which, as far as we know, is not possessed by other species: the capacity to intellectualize its conduct towards others and thereby create ethics.

It is from the basis of this principle of autonomy that we can derive our major principle, which is essential for educational practice, that pupils should always be regarded as an end in themselves and never as a means to an end. Because of this principle we should not use pupils to propagate or preserve a particular doctrine but should be concerned with developing their ability to make their own judgements and decisions. We should be attempting to lead them towards independence.

It is now a matter of choosing the appropriate method to achieve this purpose. Clearly, we should avoid such devices as indoctrination, bias, and authoritarian teaching but much depends on what we mean by these terms. In Chapter 8 we shall examine the concept of indoctrination but here we will look at impartiality, neutrality, and bias.

In attempting to lead pupils to independence, we must do certain things. We give them essential information; this means not only giving them information but also showing them different ways of looking at the facts, showing them different points of view, and trying to develop in them the ability to recognize the point of view appropriate to the circumstances. We also need to show them how different interpretations can be developed from the same point of view, and how we can critically examine these interpretations.

IMPARTIALITY

It is often claimed that a teacher should be impartial when presenting different interpretations of the facts in controversial areas such as politics and religion. What does it mean to be impartial in practice? We have seen that when we make a judgement within a specific situation we do so from a particular point of view. We first must decide which is the appropriate point of view in the circumstances. In the example which we gave of the robbery, in which an old woman had her handbag snatched, we had to decide whether to regard it from a technical or a moral point of view. The neutral facts were then given their meaning by reference to the standards appropriate to the different points of view. Generally, we would assume that it would be appropriate for the outsider to look at the neutral facts from the moral point of view. However, if we consider the robbers, they have already taken into account the moral iniquity of their action and have ruled it out. Presumably, if they had a de-briefing session after the robbery, they would be concerned only with the technical aspects of the robbery and not the moral.

Has the question of impartiality already arisen for a teacher who desires to make a salient point about the robbery? Should the teacher argue that we should consider equally the moral and technical points of view? One answer would be 'no', because the social and ethical aspects of the situation being considered are far more important than the technical aspects. This would seem to be the case but only because, in our use of language, we have put the neutral facts into the moral sphere. We have used the word 'robbery' to describe the event and that word has connotations of immorality and illegality. The event itself has pressurized us into looking at it in a certain way. Even the robbers would consciously have to rule out the moral point of view before reviewing the technical aspects.

We can look at events from different points of view but in some cases the facts themselves push us in certain directions, so that it would be inappropriate to look at the facts in a different way. Our argument here is that we would not be acting partially if we were to view the event from a moral point of view. However, in some cases, we would be acting partially if we insisted on viewing the facts from only one point of view. It is a matter of argument and the feel of the situation that lead us to decide what is appropriate. For example, Proudhon's critique of legal justice, by reference to a wider concept of social justice, was appropriate in order to indicate how, in practice, the positive law tended to favour the 'haves' rather than the 'have nots', and to emphasize the point that legal justice should not be completely separated from actual justice.[1] However, if we were giving a formal description of the law, such a manoeuvre might not be appropriate. Essentially, the task of the teacher is to help to highlight all of the relevant and appropriate arguments, and to show why they are relevant and appropriate.

The teacher must attempt to develop the skill of the pupils in distinguishing between different points of view: to recognize, for instance, that, as in the case of the robbery, we may be able to look at an event from either the technical point of view or the moral. We have also argued that the standards appropriate to a particular point of view are applied to the neutral facts and give meaning to the neutral facts. They tell us which fact is relevant or irrelevant from that point of view. However, there could well be a further problem; within a particular point of view, it is possible that the standards may differ, that different standards may be upheld, while seeming to use the same words and expressions. We shall give an example to illustrate this phenomenon.

Let us take the moral point of view and look at the concept of social or distributive justice. This is concerned with the principle by which we can distribute amongst the members of a community the benefits and burdens of belonging to that community. We can see that there could be many principles of distributive justice: we could distribute according to rank, need, desert, etc. Let us take Aristotle's concept of distributing according to desert. It would follow that if two people deserve the same they will receive the same amounts, and if they deserve differently they will receive different amounts. Aristotle accepts Plato's definition of political justice that equals should be treated equally and unequals unequally.

The first question which we need to ask is, what is the basis for deciding that some people are equal and some are not? The answer is that they each will have certain attributes which either do or do not contribute to the well-being of the community, and on that basis we will give them their deserts. The next question which we need to ask is, what kind of attribute are we talking about? Aristotle's answer is that we should look for certain virtues which will be of particular benefit to the community and then use these to assess a person's desert. We are thus deciding on the criteria for the assessment. We need to discover the virtues that would be of particular use to the Greek city state. Presumably courage is important, as the ideal state should be self-sufficient and would need to be defended. Plato put great stress on the wise, and Aristotle on the person of practical wisdom, so wisdom would be important. Aristotle's notion of corrective justice was under the general notion of equality where, for instance, the buyer and the seller should receive equal amounts: really a notion of honesty. Aristotle, in the Nicomachean Ethics, continually mentions the right action as being neither of excess or of too little but of just the right amount: really a notion of temperance.[2] Therefore, we have the following criteria of desert: courage, wisdom, honesty, and temperance.

126

By discussing the importance of each virtue for the community, we are providing a justification for their inclusion within those criteria. In the way that we have done it, by referring to Plato and Aristotle, it seems as if our justification is provided by authority. However, the real justification for Aristotle would be provided by reference to the conventions and traditions of the particular community with which we were concerned. The values that were chosen would depend on how successful the arguments were in showing how a particular virtue was important for the well-being of the community. Likewise, the virtues would need to be set up in rank order or weighted, so that they could be used to discriminate to an even greater extent between different people. Another feature of the process is that the virtues chosen and their weighting would be optional alternatives, depending on how well each virtue had been argued for and accepted. It can also be seen that, over a period of time, the particular virtues that were used as criteria of desert could change, and also that different communities could believe that other virtues were important. It could also be the case that a community could reject the idea of using virtues as criteria of desert and look for other criteria, or even that the community could reject the idea of desert as the basis for their principle of distribution.

The teacher must encourage pupils to look at not only the formal structure of principles but also the criteria and rules used in their application, to examine their justifications, and also to consider alternatives.

It is important that pupils be shown how to develop arguments and arrive at conclusions. People in a political argument do not just assess the strengths and weaknesses of arguments and then choose the most intellectually satisfying. In politics, people are often pursuing a particular interest and they will therefore be concerned with finding the best arguments which will support their attempt to pursue that interest. The teacher thus needs to show the pupils how this is done. The best way to do this is by example, that is, by demonstrating personally how the teacher would pursue certain interests and would use specific arguments and facts to support those interests. Of course, the teacher would need to reveal the nature of the interests and any related commitments and show why he/she had such interests and had developed such commitments. A teacher cannot always take the neutral chair but must often enter the situation and teach, and show how arguments are

127

used to persuade people to act in certain ways. Political arguments do not consist merely of chunks of information which are to be absorbed and understood but are action-oriented and are designed to move people in certain directions. If we are concerned with political education, and not just with the examination of all the arguments that are produced with reference to a particular issue, then it is necessary to demonstrate how arguments and evidence are used to further political ends.

As we have argued before, it is a mistake to liken a political community to an academic community, in which there is a desire to achieve some political truth and so all arguments are given equal attention in order that the nearest approximation to that truth may be achieved. Politics is about moving people in a desired direction, serving interests, and getting things done. A major part of political education must be not only to show how this is done but also to develop the skills and knowledge so that the pupils can accomplish it themselves.

It is this requirement, that the teacher should show how arguments are used to further political ends, which worries many liberal educationalists. In particular, they dislike the fact that people can have partial interests and strongly held political commitments. However, the requirement of impartiality surely requires that each individual has the right to be heard. It does not involve giving each argument the same value and therefore the same weight. Indeed, it is surely the task of the teacher to indicate the strengths of certain arguments, rather than others, and perhaps the anti-social nature of certain arguments, rather than others.

Quite clearly, political actors will disagree about the right standards to apply, about what is good and what is bad, and about how different people should be treated. Their interests may clash and so may their values. The actors will be in conflict and we therefore need a decision procedure to resolve the conflict. The procedure is the procedure of politics. It enshrines the notion of respect for others, which means that their views will be listened to, and it is acceptable to the participants: it is legitimate. It also includes the notion that the good of all should in some way be pursued: it is concerned with the public interest.

In legal terms, politics is enshrined under the notion of the rule of law, and its associated concepts of freedom under the law, and freedom of access to the law. The rule of law includes the notion of impartiality and universality: that laws should not favour or disfavour any particular individual or group but should apply equally to all non-assignable individuals. In other words, they should be universal. In the case of a dispute, or where the law has been broken, a fair trial will take place. The case will be heard fairly by an impartial judge, who will look at all the evidence and come to an unbiased decision.

The concept of the rule of law is an essential part of liberal ideology, with the two notions of impartiality and universality a major part of the whole concept. It follows that we should expect these two notions to be emphasized in liberal education and also to be major values that are recognized and used by political educators. However, the question arises as to whether there are justifications for impartiality and universality over and above the argument that they are an important part of liberal ideology. The traditional liberal defence of impartiality, which is based on the ethical idea that human beings, as potentially autonomous individuals, have the right to be treated equally, also points to an epistemological justification of impartiality.

JUSTIFICATIONS FOR IMPARTIALITY

We have seen that a traditional liberal defence of impartiality is based on the ethical notion of autonomy and individuality. It is claimed that we should treat people as ends in themselves rather than as a means to an end. It would follow from this that we should at least listen to people's points of view and properly consider their arguments. We should take their views into account when coming to a decision. This idea fits in very well with our notion of politics but it also emphasizes the point that the liberal ideal of autonomy and the associated ideal of the political way of going about things are sectarian ideas, and are therefore only one idea of the nature of human beings and their relationship with each other. It is a particular view of human beings, of their relationships, and of the good life that leads to the argument that they have universal application. This defence of impartiality is circular, since it is based on a particular ethical notion of human beings which includes within itself the idea of autonomous humans acting universally and impartially. As we have stated, the view also points to an epistemological justification that is more satisfactory. There seem to be three epistemological justifications available and each one is dependent on our concept about the nature of knowledge.

1   The objective justification   In order to make the most rational decision, we must listen to all of the arguments. It is also possible to examine arguments for consistency and coherence, and we are able to check whether factual evidence is either true or false. In ethical reasoning it is possible to transcend our own prejudices and look at things from a standpoint that is independent of ourselves and that takes account of the interests of others. We can act impersonally and look at things from the universal point of view and are therefore able to be completely objective.

The argument from the ethical point of view assumes the possibility of an autonomous, rational being who can act impersonally and make universal decisions. It is a concept of human beings in the Kantian/noumenal world. When we act impartially we are confirming our status as autonomous individuals but the epistemological achievement is also the reason why we wish to become autonomous. It provides the justification for a desire to be autonomous, since, in so doing, we are indicating that we can act objectively and impartially, and be moral.

2   Epistemological libertarianism, or the subjectivist justification for impartiality   It is based on the notion that truth is not attainable and that morality is relative. In Kantian terms, it is the recognition that we also live in the phenomenal world, but with the depressing conclusion that we cannot get out of it.

The line of reasoning is as follows. The truth is not attainable, so we have to rely on our own commitments or inter-subjective commitments. However, we know that our commitments, no matter how strong they may be, cannot provide a justification for the propositions that we put forward. They cannot guarantee the truth of the propositions; our commitments are merely subjective feelings and we cannot rely on subjective or inter-subjective feelings. Indeed, the conclusion must be that all of our truth claims are baseless. We have no independent criteria of truth which we can rely on, so our beliefs and our arguments are all worthless. There is no reason why we should not give an equal weight to all beliefs and arguments. It follows from this that we can be completely impartial and treat all arguments with the same contempt. Such a stance also precludes action because there is no point in acting on baseless ideas which are merely expressions of our feelings. In any case, we have no way of knowing whether one decision is better than another decision. Impartiality is the only intellectual position that we can honestly hold because no argument can be more intellectually attractive than any other. It also follows that there is no point in listening to the different arguments in an attempt to arrive at a decision, since it would merely involve the swapping of prejudices.

The libertarian epistemology is very different from the liberal position of John Stuart Mill, who saw the political process as part of the pursuit of truth, and the listening to all argument as a necessary step in its attainment.[3] This modern-day epistemological libertarianism is a philosophy of despair, and would destroy the basis of politics as a rational and ethical pursuit. It opens the way to the pursuit of mere power and to the exercise of force. Indeed, we could reverse the whole argument and say that, on the same basis, there is no reason to be impartial, as there is no rational justification for impartiality. We might as well be biased. It just depends on our commitments or on any whim that we may have at any particular time.

3 The pragmatic justification for impartiality   This recognizes that the gaining of knowledge must have a personal element in it, and that, if we were to have the ability to be purely objective, we would need to be a creature acting outside space and time. As Kant pointed out, each of us is a creature of desires and passions who has the capacity to struggle beyond their hold and to strive for something more universal and impersonal. However, we can never achieve certainty nor be purely objective. Our knowledge is uncertain and is based on our fallible power of judgement, which, in its turn arises from within a vast framework of previous judgements, prejudices, experiences, and half-understood ideas and concepts. In a sense, where the Kantian moral legislator aspires to a God-like status, this moral legislator clearly recognizes self-limitations and yet still struggles to achieve objectivity. (We could argue that the God-like moral legislator and the person struggling to achieve objectivity are both elements in Kant's thought.) Under this argument, we must define objectivity in such a way that it may be achieved rather than placed beyond the range of human achievement.

Our attempt to be objective lies in putting our thoughts into the public arena so that they can be discussed, examined, criticized, agreed with, or rejected. It lies in using language and concepts that can be understood by other people. It is lies in freezing ideas so that they no longer rely on our own support, commitment, and passion but are independent. They are then assessed in the public arena by our peers. These notions of ideas being expressed in the public arena, being independent, and being publicly assessed are essential features of objectivity. The achievement of objectivity is a public achievement, since all ideas, if they are going to have any standing, must pass through the gamut of public investigation. The very process of achieving objectivity demands that all ideas should be given a fair hearing in the search for truth, and that the tentative nature of truth points to care in ruling out outrageous or strange concepts. The nature of our understanding and of our truth claims demand that all ideas, if put in a proper form (a form accessible to the public), have a right to be considered.

Just as a person has a right to be heard as a member of the language community, so an idea has a right to be considered if it exists within the public domain. In the public domain it can be considered impersonally. The impartial person who is presiding has a duty to allow a person to speak and a duty to prepare the ground for the fair hearing of the idea, whatever the status of the speaker. For example, an idea should be rejected not because it is the idea of a racist but because in the public domain it fails to meet the criteria related to its truth.

We believe that the third justification for impartiality is the most sound, as it is consistent with our general argument about the nature of knowledge and our understanding of it.

THE NEUTRAL CHAIRPERSON

Joan Ruddock[4] sets out four requirements for a chairperson, who is also a teacher:

1   The teacher should not use his/her authority as a teacher to promote a personal view.
2   In controversial areas, the mode of enquiry should chiefly be through discussion rather than instruction.
3   The chairperson should ensure that the discussion will promote and protect a divergence of views amongst the participants in the discussion.

4 The chairperson, as a teacher, has a responsibility to maintain quality and standards in learning.

The general point is that a teacher, when a controversial issue arises, should treat all opinions equally and completely and, of course, should not express a personal viewpoint.

The first requirement is acceptable if we assume that the word 'authority' is being used in the sense of being 'in authority'. If the teacher is 'an authority' on a certain issue, we would presumably hope that he/she would express a personal opinion with the necessary argument and evidence. We would expect the teacher to present the evidence fairly, in the sense that he/she should not conceal evidence or exaggerate supporting evidence. The argument would need to be put in such a way that the pupils could see the strength of the evidence and the argument and be able to assess it for themselves. It could even be argued that, being a teacher first and a chairperson second, the teacher should declare his/her interest and indicate the direction to which the evidence points. This is important because the pupils must be able not only to understand what counts as evidence but also to see and understand the process of reaching conclusions. We have seen previously how rational argument can continue to take place even when there is an agreement about the facts. The pupils must be shown how this can be so in order that they may eventually be able to produce such arguments themselves.

Of course, in practice, when dealing with a controversial issue, the teacher must know when to enter the fray in order to widen and perhaps develop the discussion. It may also be possible for the teacher to state that he/she has views on a particular issue and will reveal these views at a later stage in the proceedings. Any teacher who has attempted to act as a neutral chairperson will know that the pupils desire to hear the teacher's viewpoint and will actually ask the teacher for an opinion. To state that one will not tell them is a peculiar response and turns the proceedings into a silly guessing game. It would also seem rather odd if one insisted that one had no views and remained neutral on a highly charged controversial issue, which was supposed to be of concern to everyone, particularly as the whole point of looking at controversial issues is to lead people to an interest in matters of public concern.

It would also seem to be the function of the teacher to

guide a discussion away from the mere swapping of prejudices and to ask for evidence and argument from different stances if they fail to appear. Indeed, this would seem to be a prerequisite if the teacher is to fulfil the responsibility to maintain quality and standards. This could be a problem because conclusions are very much bound up with the values and viewpoints that a person holds; the laying bare of an argument can often greatly weaken its emotive force and destroy its strength. However, should this not be the task of the teacher, if it is not achieved by the participants in the discussion? If a skilful debater successfully persuades the participants in a discussion about race that the views of the National Front on such an issue are correct, should not the teacher come in and at least attempt to persuade the participants that the argument may be weaker than they thought?[5] After all, the original aim of holding the discussion was to achieve some educational goal; if it blatantly fails to do this, then the teacher must surely step down as chairperson and act as teacher.

It would follow from this that it must also be the teacher's task to introduce views that have not been expressed, and arguments and evidence which support or disagree with views that have been expressed but have not been considered adequately. J. Wellington asks whether neutrality or balance is important and asks which should take precedence.[6] Our answer is that it is the function of the neutral teacher, although perhaps not the neutral chairperson, to see that all views, with arguments and evidence, are presented and that their strengths and weaknesses are examined. A teacher who is using discussion as a teaching method, and is therefore acting as a neutral chairperson, has a duty to be more active in guiding a discussion and in making sure that viewpoints are introduced and arguments put forward, than a non-teacher. The discussion is being introduced not for its own sake but as a teaching method to explore issues and to see how justificatory arguments are developed and decisions reached. The hope is that pupils will eventually be able to make informed judgements based on a full consideration of the arguments and evidence, rather than uninformed judgements based on prejudice and emotions. It is also hoped that, although each viewpoint is to be given a full and fair hearing, the pupils will come to recognize that some arguments are weak and that others are strong.

BIAS

In political and moral discussions, to declare that a view shows bias is an indication that the person making the declaration believes that the person who is considering evidence or making a decision has been influenced by certain beliefs, which are not acceptable to the observer, and is giving the wrong weighting to evidence and argument. The word 'bias', as well as being a pejorative term, indicates that something is deviating from the right track, that a decision is not in accordance with the appropriate standard, that the arguments accepted as strong are weak or unacceptable.

We could say that the beliefs that have wrongly influenced the biased actor are unacceptable because they are unreasonable, irrational, based on misguided ideology, or based on a collection of doubtful theories.

Unreasonable beliefs

Something is unreasonable if it is not based on our usual canons of common sense. There are certain procedures which would be considered reasonable and certain criteria by which we may judge reasonableness. We can assess the reasonableness of an argument in two ways. A person's train of thought may be made accessible through public language. If it is not made accessible in such a way and if questions are answered not with argument and evidence but with phrases such as 'I know', 'I know by intuition', 'I feel in my bones', then we can surmise that the reason for a decision or the acceptance of an argument is not open to public scrutiny and is therefore probably not sound. If an argument or decision does become public and is open to public scrutiny, we can check it by tests which are appropriate to the subject in question. For instance, utterances that did not satisfy the basic rules of language would be considered unreasonable, so it would be necessary for a reasonable argument at least to satisfy such rules. However, an argument that met these criteria would still be unreasonable if it ignored accepted procedures for judging or testing something. For instance, an argument indicating that a person was judging the weight of some material by its size, without taking into account its mass, would be considered unreasonable. In order to check an argument for its reasonableness, we could ask certain standard questions about the form of the argument. For instance, is the argument internally consistent; does it receive support from the factual evidence or does it seem to contradict it; if it contradicts the evidence, would that seem to be good grounds for rejecting it? More contentiously, is a generalization derived from an acceptable number of instances? For example, it would be unreasonable to say that all swans are white after seeing only one swan. It would be less unreasonable to say that all swans are white after seeing a hundred swans, and even less so to say that most swans are white after seeing a hundred swans. It would be reasonable to say that, since we have seen only a hundred swans, we cannot say that all swans are white. However, would it be reasonable to say that we have seen only eight million swans and that all are white but nevertheless we cannot say that all swans are white? It would probably be unreasonable but correct and the caution very wise. In spite of that, a scientist who repeated the same experiment eight million times and always obtained the same result but nevertheless felt that the same experiment should be continued in case one day a different result were achieved would be considered not only unreasonable but also mad. (However, remember our previous point, that an argument that ignored accepted procedures for judging or testing something would be unreasonable. Would a scientist who ignored Popperian methodology be considered unreasonable by everyone or only by a Popperian?) It would be reasonable to base our decision on our previous experience, no matter how small, if we were with a group where no one but ourselves had any experience. In the scientific arena, it would be reasonable for the scientific community to base its decision as to the worth of a new theory on the experience of associated theories in the same field, as well as on the factual evidence and the actual arguments of the discovering scientist. It would be reasonable because the scientific community would be the proper body to make the decision. It is the accepted decision-making body for science and therefore could legitimately make the decision. Nevertheless, it could make a reasonable but wrong decision.

It can be seen that we can make a reasonable decision that is correct, a reasonable decision that is incorrect, a reasonable decision by refusing to make a decision; we can be unreasonable and incorrect, or unreasonable and correct. In other words, there is no necessary connection between the reasonableness or unreasonableness of a decision or an argument and its correctness. Nevertheless, the hope is that a reasonable decision or argument, which takes into account the relevant evidence and arguments, is more likely to be correct than decisions or arguments that do not do so.

To act reasonably is usually associated with an attempt to act for the sake of fairness or the truth. To act unreasonably is usually associated with not taking much notice of the evidence and with favouring one person or group over another for no good reason.

Irrational beliefs

It would be simpler if we applied the term 'irrational' only to arguments and beliefs; in that sense, an act could only be unreasonable, although it could be based on an irrational belief. An argument is irrational if it does not follow the rules of logic; for instance, if we failed to follow the law of contradiction that something cannot be 'p' and 'not p' at the same time. Of course, in practice, it may be that we recognize the illogicality of a certain argument but go along with it because we are committed to support a certain individual or group. However, this would indicate that we are biased but would not be absolute proof because, as far as the observer knows, we may be too stupid to recognize the illogicality of the argument. This also raises the question as to whether we need to be intentionally biased if we are going to be considered biased at all. In such a case, we could say that a stupid person's decision is biased, as there are no good reasons for it (failure to understand an argument would presumably not count as a good reason), but the person is not biased.

We could say that someone is acting on an irrational belief if they continue to believe something in spite of very good evidence to the contrary. For example a person believes the Earth is flat and makes a decision, whether or not to support a particular exploration, on the basis of such a belief. Another example, which is also concerned with factual evidence rather than the logic of arguments, is when people continue to do something in spite of the evidence of their senses, which indicate that they would be foolish to do so. For example, soldiers walk into a hail of machine-gun bullets, after the group before them have all been shot dead, in the belief that they will not be hurt. In this case, they hold a previous false belief which, before their eyes, is again falsified but they reject all immediate evidence of their senses because of a strong belief that their case is different from the other soldiers or that patriotism provides a special protection to the flesh.

Thus it can be seen that we can be irrational on three grounds: we fail to recognize the rules of logic; we fail to take into account the evidence of our senses; we fail to take into account the vast weight of scientific evidence. In the last two cases, we could be irrational but right.[7]

Beliefs based on a misguided ideology

1   People have a misguided ideology if we believe that they have no good reason for holding such a belief. We believe that they are acting unreasonably, and probably irrationally, in holding such a belief.
2   People have an ideology which we consider may be all right for them but which goes against our own set of beliefs about human beings and their relationship to others. In other words, our position is relative; most ideologies are all right but we are committed to ours and they are committed to theirs. When our interests clash, we know that they must be judging events from the point of view of their ideology and that therefore they are biased.
3   We believe that to follow any ideology is mistaken and that it is possible to look at facts neutrally and impartially. We can relate this to our objective justification of impartiality.

An ideology is an abridgement of a tradition and is thus a distortion. It is a collection of principles and beliefs that are cut off from practice and therefore it lacks reality and cannot be used effectively. Following such a line of argument, Edmund Burke pointed out that during the French Revolution the revolutionaries took what they saw as the principles of English political practice and tried to apply them in France. They failed because political practice is not a matter of applying principles but consists of half-formed principles, values, skills, abilities, practices, and prejudices which are particularly related to the time and the place of the practice.

It follows that an ideology is an attempt at providing a systematic group of principles and values, whereas political practice is neither systematic nor entirely dependent on principles and values. The argument would therefore be that we would be biased if we followed an ideology but not biased if we did not. This is an interesting argument because it rules out unconscious bias as being bias at all. Presumably if we consciously built up our framework and judged things in accordance with it, we could be accused of conscious bias; if we simply judged things in accordance with the framework that we happened to have, in the way that the Burkean argument suggests, we could not be accused of conscious bias. (However, no doubt sociologists could state that we showed unconscious bias.)

The argument also provides us with two criticisms of what we have called the objective justification for impartiality. First, within the tacit framework of our understanding, we would not be able to achieve pure objectivity; second, if we did associate the objective justification with liberalism, we would be pointing to its ideological character. The reason for this, as we have seen, is that pure objectivity is not attainable. The concept exists because we have withdrawn from practice certain notions that we are trying to bring about, have formed them into a group of principles and values, and have mistakenly regarded them as if they are realizable in themselves. We have, in a sense, created an ideology, that is, a collection of principles and values distinct from practice. The use of the combined objective/liberal approach to judge things would therefore be an indication that we were using an ideology as our framework and that we were biased.

4 Our final problem is to consider whether or not we could avoid the accusation of bias if we combined our pragmatic justification for impartiality with the practice of politics. We think that we could, although the argument does not seem to be clear cut. The pragmatic justification for impartiality is a picture of our attempt to achieve objectivity in the real world. We remain within practice and do not attempt to withdraw the principles and values from practice. It is not prescriptive but is an attempt to explain how we approach an understanding of nature and experience and communicate it to others. On the other hand, the objective approach is really a formalization of our hopes and aspirations. It is a withdrawal of half-formed concepts from practice. Our attempt to understand is our first attempt at objectivity, whereas pure objectivity is a refinement, an intellectual sifting out of the pieces of humanity that prevent its attainment. It creates an unattainable ideal but

is nevertheless something that we strive to achieve because the closer we come to achieving it then the greater our understanding and the more public our knowledge. Likewise, it could be argued that politics is about practice. It is an explanation of how people sometimes attempt to behave when they are struggling to raise social relationships above mere power relations and to include an ethical or a human element in those relationships. It is the following of procedures which avoid naked power and point to peaceful resolutions that reflect human dignity. Liberalism, or at least ethical liberalism, can be regarded as an idealized version of these procedures: a withdrawal of half-formed practices and ideals, and the formulation of them into a system of procedures and relationships that are clear cut and attractive but are probably unattainable. The pragmatic approach to objectivity and politics has arisen after many years of struggle and intellectual achievement in the real world. It has evolved. Pure objectivity and liberalism have arisen through a contemplation of their development. They are a pure intellectualization of the activities but nevertheless, once formulated, they have helped in their development.

Our argument is that our combined pragmatic/political approach is not ideological in the sense that we have used the term. Of course, in arguing this, it can be seen that we do not entirely accept the Burkean perspective. We think that it is too pessimistic about the nature of human beings and their potential and that, even if humans cannot achieve objectivity and the complete epistemological justification for objectivity, they should at least try. The political approach is a symptom of their trying, and the possibility of not being biased and of acting ethically is a hope. We fit them together with our pragmatic justification of impartiality, while recognizing that Burke and his ilk may well be right.

Beliefs based on a collection of doubtful theories

The argument here is that we can surely be condemned as being biased if we are intentionally using theories that we know to be false as a basis for deciding on the standing of other arguments. For instance, we should be biased if we, as neo-Mendelian Darwinians, were to use Lamarckian theories to judge the value of a modern-day biologist's work. It would be unusual to accuse someone of bias if they used accepted scientific knowledge as a basis for estimating the worth of new theories, even if we accepted the argument that scientific knowledge is only tentative. In other words, we can be successfully accused of bias only if we are consciously allowing some eccentric ideas to influence our decision as to the worth of new theories or evidence. However, if we really believe that the eccentric ideas are true or are the proper basis for estimating the worth of the new theory or evidence then, although we could be accused of bias, it would be difficult to substantiate the accusation.

CONCLUSION

We have argued that the need to treat people impartially is desirable from the ethical notion of treating people as ends in themselves rather than as means to an end. As unique rational agents, we should take account of their views and give them a fair hearing. This is also related to the notion of social justice. It is a requirement of justice that we should take account of everyone's interests and their contribution to the community. In order to achieve this, we must allow individuals to put forward their interests and express their claims.

We have also argued that it is a requirement of rationality that people are allowed to put forward many different viewpoints so that a full and fair consideration be given to each argument. However, impartiality does not require us to give equal weighting to all viewpoints but leads us to examine the strengths and weaknesses of the different arguments.

We also looked at the role of the teacher/chairperson. We indicated that it is part of the role of the teacher to show how arguments are used and conclusions reached but that the teacher also has a role, like a judge, to bring out relevant arguments and evidence and to lead the discussion to the most reasonable conclusion. This is connected to the relationship between impartiality, impersonality, universality, and objectivity. We impartially examine the evidence and arguments in order to achieve the most rational decision, that which ideally would be universally agreed. (Of course, it is possible to have more than one rational decision amply supported by arguments and evidence, as shown by appeal court decisions in which judges produce minority and majority decisions. This emphasizes why we need to have recognized procedures for resolving disputes rather than relying on the hope that there is only one rational decision.) The rational decision ideally is impersonal, in the sense that it is related to the argument and evidence rather than to the characteristics of the person or persons putting forward the evidence. This is also the epistemological justification for impartiality, as it is a necessary step in the achievement of objectivity.

Bias is a pejorative term, suggesting that we are being influenced by some beliefs for no good reason. It differs from partiality in the sense that we could be partial to something for a good reason and therefore would not be open to such criticism. For instance, we might talk of someone as being partial to the truth but not as being biased towards the truth. When we are impartial, we are concerned with objectivity and with obtaining the truth; when we are biased, we are concerned not with the merits of the case or with the evidence but with whether the arguments or evidence can support our case or the interests of ourselves or our group.

As the word 'bias' is a pejorative term, it is usually used to indicate that someone is consciously misusing the evidence and arguments. However, it is also commonly used to vilify the judgements and decisions of people who are believed to be motivated by opinions that we consider to be misguided. As this is the case, it is extremely difficult for a participant in an argument to believe that an adversary is impartial. A relativist would also argue that everyone is biased in favour of their own views. A complete justification for impartiality must move beyond an ethical justification to an epistemological justification, which has to come from an objectivist stance or rather from what we have called the pragmatic justification for impartiality.

Chapter eight

INDOCTRINATION

Most opposition to the inclusion of political education in the curriculum comes from those who maintain that the teaching of politics in schools would be the first stepping-stone to political indoctrination. It is generally alleged that, although the boundary between education and indoctrination can be maintained, there are particular areas of study where that boundary becomes blurred. Two of these 'danger areas' are politics and religion.

Anyone who believes that political education should be taught in schools must allay the fears of those who see dangers of indoctrination as a serious impediment to the teaching of politics. There are a number of questions which must be addressed. Some of these relate to the nature of indoctrination itself. What kind of factors and conditions would need to operate before a satisfactory system of indoctrination could be introduced? Which of these factors, if any, would be accentuated by the introduction of politics into schools? Other questions relate to the extent and function of indoctrination. We generally accept that politics is a 'danger zone' as far as indoctrination is concerned, but are there other areas which are equally susceptible? When we speak of 'political indoctrination', do we mean 'politics' with a large or small 'p'? Recent attempts at mapping the 'logical geography' of educational concepts have been equally prolific in providing the main constituents of indoctrination. These analyses may provide a useful starting point for tackling some of the problems that arise from an examination of indoctrination. However, it might be useful to begin our examination of indoctrination by providing a brief historical introduction.

The fear of indoctrination dominated many of those who were concerned with education in the nineteenth century. By the middle of the century it was becoming clear that charitable and religious institutions were not likely to have sufficient resources for providing a universally free system of education. The only way forward seemed to be by means of government intervention and support on a large scale. This presented those concerned with promoting a universal system of education with a number of problems. Government intervention in education could only be bad: 'An attempt to replace an independent system of education by a compulsory system managed by the Government would be met by objections - both religious and political.'[1] Other countries had introduced education under government control but this would be unacceptable to the vast majority of Britons.

It was the 'religious question' that gave rise to the greatest controversy. No progress could be made on the setting-up of state education unless some kind of compromise could be reached on the form that religious instruction would take in elementary schools. All sects agreed that 'religious truth' should be taught. Most objected to 'sectarian dogma' but could not agree on what was to count as 'religious truth' and what was 'dogma'. Rather than embark on acrimonious discussions on the difference between 'dogma' and 'truth', a purely pragmatic solution was adopted. Those parts of Christian teaching that were acceptable to all became 'truths' to be taught in elementary schools. The teaching that belonged to particular sects was 'dogma' and was taught in denominational schools, which received financial support from their particular churches. However, there was much suspicion concerning the Anglican Church in its role as the established church. It could use its position to attain what might be called an unfair religious advantage. Thus, the fears that people had were expressed in terms of one sect having the means of 'exerting an unfair influence' or 'exerting influence on impressionable minds'.

There are those who suggest that all education is indoctrination and others who assert that indoctrination is not necessarily bad or that it is possible to distinguish between 'good' and 'bad' indoctrination. The notion that all education is indoctrination is based on the assumption that what we call 'socialization', or bringing up children with a particular way of life or ethos, is always indoctrination. Bertrand Russell expressed this view to some extent when he wrote: 'In all education, propaganda has a part. The question for the educator is not whether there shall be propaganda - but how much, how organised, and of what sort?' However, Russell believed that this could be alleviated by encouraging children to use their critical faculties 'by teaching them methods of arriving at impartial judgements'.[2]

It is doubtful whether those who say that all education is indoctrination would be assured by Russell's point. They would insist that even the way in which we go about criticizing things is in itself a form of indoctrination. Although it is true that we cannot escape from the cultural background in which we have been brought up, it is equally true, however, that we cannot think, critically or uncritically, without some kind of framework. Those who insist that all education is indoctrination resemble those people who insist that from the moment of our birth we are approaching the day of our death. In that sense we are all 'dying' but such 'dying' would not entitle us to a bed in a hospice for the terminally ill.

That we choose to talk of 'indoctrination' as a kind of activity to be avoided is only because it seems to conflict with particular values and assumptions. A society which did not hold these views would be unperturbed by what we call indoctrination. It might be useful to examine what these values are and what the conflicts are which give rise to 'indoctrination'.

The notion of indoctrination arises chiefly in religion. Originally the term 'indoctrination' meant little more than 'immersed in' or 'thoroughly grounded in' but it became necessary to distinguish between methods of teaching religion which were legitimate and those which were regarded as illegitimate. Some religions seemed to have more difficulties than others. The notion that 'this person has accepted the Christian faith and that's all there is to it' would not have sufficed in all cases. The question, 'how did the person come to believe?', was of importance. The protestant forms of religion laid great emphasis on the individual conscience. To some extent, the priest could not covert a person to the faith. This could be achieved only by the individual's conscience. Thus, conversion meant 'self-conversion' or 'conversion following one's own conscience'. Any conversion that was not accomplished in such a way would be regarded with suspicion. Any society purporting to support freedom of conscience, freedom of religious belief as deeply held values would run into the kind of difficulties that tend to be subsumed under 'indoctrination'. The desire to bring someone into a set of beliefs had to be weighed against other deeply held beliefs, i.e. liberty of conscience and freedom of religious belief. The problem could be solved only by a kind of balancing act. The term 'indoctrination' became a useful term to employ when it was suspected that something had gone wrong with this balancing act.

The accusation of indoctrination is usually accompanied by phrases, 'in religion, in politics, in ideology'. This seems to imply that there are particular areas of interest that are particularly prone to indoctrination. If this is the case, it may be important to examine them in some detail to try to determine what it is about them that places them within this category. Equally, having examined these categories, it might be useful to ask ourselves whether it is only religion and politics that are susceptible to indoctrination or whether indoctrination may not cover a wider range of propositions than is usually suspected.

Certain kinds of activities, such as religion and politics, seem to represent danger zones as far as indoctrination is concerned but it would obviously be wrong to insist that all teaching in these subjects is indoctrination. Whether indoctrination occurs or not depends on factors extraneous to subject matter. R.M. Hare suggested that the genuine teacher differs from those concerned with indoctrination by method and intention:

> The educator is waiting and hoping all the time for those whom he is educating to start thinking. The indoctrinator, on the other hand, is watching for signs of trouble and ready to intervene to suppress it when it appears.[3]

The teacher is concerned with the intellectual and moral growth of the pupil; the indoctrinator is not.

John Wilson is not convinced by such arguments, however.[4] He feels that indoctrination is connected with the kind of proposition. A method of instruction which might obviously be indoctrination in one situation would not be suspect in another: sleep-learning mathematical tables, however undesirable, in some respects would certainly not be regarded as indoctrination. He is also doubtful whether indoctrination could occur in physics. If pupils could be taught A-level physics by having an electrode passed through their brain, it would be purely arbitrary whether or not we would call this indoctrination.

Wilson sees the indoctrinator as one who trades in faulty logic and faulty evidence. Indoctrination involves insisting on the truth and certainty of propositions that may be neither true nor certain. Indoctrination occurs when we are concerned with propositions of a particular epistemological status. Such propositions lack the status of 'truth' or 'certainty' but there may be considerable evidence in their favour. In other cases, despite some supporting evidence, there may be some evidence against them, making the supporting evidence far from conclusive. However, a teacher who wished pupils to accept such propositions would present the favourable evidence in greater detail and would omit the contrary evidence altogether. If this unfavourable evidence were not suppressed altogether, it might be presented in such a way as to discredit it.

Wilson suggests a number of ways in which he believes such indoctrination can be avoided. We should not, in our attempt to exclude indoctrination, confine ourselves to beliefs that are certain but it is important that the 'general weight of evidence' is in their favour. Such propositions 'may be certain or they may be highly probable or probable or just likely on the whole' but the crucial point is that these propositions are backed by evidence. It is also important that when we speak of evidence it is 'publicly accepted evidence, not simply what sectarians regarded as evidence'.

Prima facie, Wilson's analysis would appear to be at least sensible and non-controversial. His insistence that beliefs should be rational and backed by evidence that is 'publicly acceptable' would seem to allay suspicion. However, when we look at his advice more closely, a number of difficulties appear. Wilson does not seem to be making the point that any belief, which the vast majority hold to be rational and which is backed by 'publicly acceptable evidence', could not by definition be indoctrination. Some have indeed held that the teaching of any belief which the majority disliked could be called 'indoctrination'. This does not seem to be Wilson's position, however. He obviously believes that it will not do to make a simple demarcation between education and indoctrination on the grounds of approval and disapproval. Instead, he sees the operation broadly in terms of deliberately faulty reasoning and of the deliberate fudging or withholding of evidence required for the acceptance of a particular belief. The difficulty lies in equating 'acceptable evidence' with what is 'publicly acceptable': Galileo put forward evidence that was not generally acceptable and so it might have been called sectarian.

However, the reference to evidence for beliefs does, nonetheless, bring us to one of the crucial elements in our understanding of what is occurring in indoctrination. Outside mathematics and formal logic, where we are concerned with a tight system of deductive reasoning, the evidence for a particular proposition is always less than complete. Writers are seldom concerned about the possibility of indoctrination in mathematics. In many ways, the wedge which has been driven between 'method' and 'subject matter' is misleading. To talk of 'evidence' in mathematics is misleading: the proof of a proposition is the mathematics. That is why we might not become too disturbed if we learned that children were being taught mathematics by hypnosis. The answers to any calculations that they were taught to do under hypnosis would be the same as the answers that they would be expected to produce while wide awake. There is no room for indoctrination to manoeuvre a little pressure, a little more coercion in favour of one conclusion rather than another.

The suggestion that indoctrination could occur, wherever there is a gap between conclusion and evidence or between a belief and justification for a belief, gives rise to an important question. Could indoctrination occur outside its traditional haunts of religion and politics? Should we be on our guard, searching for indoctrination, in other areas of teaching?

R.S. Peters suggests that it might be useful to examine the notion of a doctrine. If there are 'high risk' and 'low risk' areas, a doctrine could be expected to bear the criteria of a 'high risk area'. He writes: 'Whatever else indoctrination may mean it obviously has something to do with doctrines, which are a species of belief.'[5] Even when we have provided an adequate account of the nature of a doctrine, however, it may be naive to assume that only doctrines might be indoctrinated. On the other hand, there seems to be little point in extending the word 'doctrine' to cover any proposition or belief which may be indoctrinated.

However, attempts have been made to elucidate the notion of a doctrine by applying the Verification Principle. Propositions which pass the verifiability test are not doctrines; those which do not pass the test are 'doctrines' and so are candidates for indoctrination. Some writers have made efforts along these lines but difficulties with the Verification Principle are notorious.[6] These difficulties have frequently been thought to lie in the ability of a logician to formulate the principle adequately. Obviously a rule of thumb measure was required which would include the propositions of science but exclude those of metaphysics. Somewhat perversely, any verification principle which is wide enought to include science tends also to include metaphysics.

Before we abandon the notion of verifiability, or falsifiability, it might be useful to look closely at two different notions of falsifiability. Some propositions are unfalsifiable, not because we are incapable of gathering observations, states of affairs, etc., which could falsify them, but because we refuse to allow any state of affairs to count against them. Scientists and philosophers frequently talk of hypotheses and theories as being 'refuted' by facts but, more accurately, the scientist appreciates that a particular experiment or set of observations is incompatible with his theory. Human beings put forward and develop theories and human beings appreciate when it is time to disregard those theories. Popper pointed to two theories which could not be falsified, not because of a lack of falsifying instances but because these falsifying instances were explained away. Their truth was always assured. 'It was precisely this fact, that they always fitted, that they were always confirmed - which in the eyes of their admirers constituted the strongest arguments in their favour.'[7] However, Popper saw their non-falsifiability as a weakness.

In this way, to many people, Marxism was a set of incontrovertible and unchanging truths. Not only could there be no evidence against them but it would also be politically unwise to suggest that there could be. Similarly, psycho-analysis was construed so that its tenets became a set of 'truths'. While we would have little hesitation in referring to the ideas of Marx or Lenin as 'doctrines', it is perhaps immaterial whether the theories of psychoanalysis are referred to as Freudian or Jungian doctrines, or Freudian or Jungian theories.

Once we allow that indoctrination may occur wherever alternative explanations and interpretations are logically possible, our general thinking about the kind of processes that occur in indoctrination must change to some extent. The suggestion, for example, that it is the subject matter of propositions that makes indoctrination possible, shows that indoctrination could occur outside politics and religion. If we do not feel constrained to worry about the possibility of indoctrination within the sciences, this complacency rests not on the special status of the propositions that are used in science but rather on the fact that the mechanics of scientific method are structured to avoid it. The great American philosopher, C.S. Peirce, contrasted the mechanisms of closed and open systems of reasoning. In the essay, 'The fixation of belief', he discusses what he calls 'The Method Tenacity'. He imagines that an institution is formulated with the purpose of holding particular truths before the people. These doctrines are taught to the young who learn them by heart. At the same time, the institution has 'the power to prevent contrary doctrines being taught, advocated or expressed. Let all possible cases of a change of mind be removed from man's apprehension.' This is the model upon which the indoctrinator would work. However, such systems are generally difficult to construct. Ultimately, Peirce believed, the human mind will question these beliefs. It will occur to a person that at some time the opinions of other people are equally as good. 'This conception that another man's thought and sentiment may be equivalent to one's own, is a distinctly new step and a highly important one.'[8]

If we have little anxiety about indoctrination within the physical sciences, it is because we feel that there are checks and balances within science which render this 'fixation of belief' unlikely. The very fabric of science rests on the notion that nothing should be accepted as certainly true, that science is open-ended. However, before looking at the physical sciences in more detail, it might be useful to look at some of the other characteristics of indoctrination.

The assumption that indoctrination depends upon the nature of the subject matter and the kind of proposition involved leaves us with the prospect that indoctrination could occur in activities outside the traditional danger areas of religion and politics. It should also be remembered that, even if it is granted that mathematics is a low risk area for indoctrination, indoctrination about mathematics and the nature of mathematics has frequently been of a most vicious nature. The famous demand of the Pythagoreans, that anyone revealing the irrationality of the number two should be struck dead, has passed into history. However, the ruthless suppression of those investigating the possibility of non-Euclidean geometry, as late as the nineteenth century, is less well publicized. The possibility that there could be alternative points of view to Euclid seemed to challenge the certainty of mathematics.

The areas in which indoctrination could occur seem to be wider than is often supposed and there are not particular sets of subject matter which are rendered immune. Subject matter may be an important element but it is crucial that other aspects of indoctrination should be examined.

Indoctrination is frequently described in terms such as the following. It is the inculcation of beliefs which the recipient will never question. The evidence for these beliefs will be carefully chosen and will back up the beliefs. This kind of indoctrination may occur for a number of reasons. The teacher will genuinely believe them and have fears for the soul or welfare of those rejecting these beliefs. Much religious indoctrination was doubtless of this kind. Concomitant with this religious fervour was, of course, the power aspect: if a church lost converts, it also lost power.

One of the crucial differences between indoctrination and education rests upon the different attitude towards people/pupils. It was suggested earlier that indoctrination was a genuine concern in particular kinds of society because it seemed to encroach on other deeply held values. The balance between teaching children religious beliefs, which the teachers themselves hope that the children will retain, and indoctrinating the children is no doubt a narrow one. However, side by side with the hope that the children will become practising believers is the principle, equally upheld, that the children must make up their own minds. Further, there is the belief that, without the informed consent of the person concerned, the acceptance of a set of beliefs is somehow invalidated. Broadly speaking, political systems that regard their people as 'subjects' are less concerned by the possibility of indoctrination than those who regard their people as 'citizens'.

The teacher/pupil relationship has some of the ingredients of what we call 'indoctrination'. The teacher is responsible for the welfare of the child and for teaching the child the skills and beliefs that are believed necessary for the child to possess in order to become a responsible citizen. It was the fear of indoctrination - the fear of the teacher dominating the personality of the child - which encouraged the proliferation of 'child-centred' and 'progressive' methods of education. In some cases, of course, these admirable exercises amounted to an abnegation of the teacher's responsibility.

An indoctrinator may regard the child as a receptacle to be filled with beliefs. The educator, as Hare indicates, is concerned with the growth and development of the child. The child is not a 'thing' to be filled with beliefs but a person, who has both the right and the duty of weighing up evidence and of coming to independent decisions. Although the teacher may hope that the child will embrace certain values, the teacher must also hope that these values have been accepted only after critical thought. Martin Buber has outlined the kind of relationship which could occur between teacher and pupil or doctor and patient, where the pupil or patient becomes a 'thing'.

> Consider the relationship of doctor and patient. It is essential that this should be a real human relationship... but as soon as the helper is touched with a desire, however subtle in form, to dominate, or enjoy his patient, the danger of falsification arises, besides which all quackery become peripheral.[9]

Teachers have never been called upon to sign any document resembling the Hippocratic Oath. Nevertheless, it is assumed that teachers have a duty to teach what we might call 'the truth', or to initiate pupils into the knowledge of the day, to the best of their ability. In this sense, the word 'truth' is used lightly because no teacher can seriously believe that the present state of knowledge represents the last word on the matter. However, a physics teacher may be confident that teaching the law of gravitation, as propounded by Newton, is not leading pupils astray, despite the later work of Einstein. Part of a teacher's undertaking, as far as knowledge is concerned, may well be to say something about the epistemological status of what is being taught; that is, that knowledge changes and for that reason it is important to try to understand the evidence which we have for believing any particular theory that we have at the moment. This approach is far removed from relativism, where the general notion seems to be that, unless there is conclusive evidence, there can be no evidence at all and therefore one belief is as good as any other.

Despite the efforts of a few teachers to play down or to avoid the teaching situation, it is generally assumed that teachers do know more than their pupils and that they have a duty of passing on this knowledge accurately. Whether they think of themselves as a teacher or a 'facilitator' depends no doubt on what and where they are teaching. In some cases at least, teachers have the opportunity of 'pulling a fast one' in favour of one belief or theory rather than another, but the teacher-pupil relationship seems to forbid this.

Indoctrination therefore seems to bring us into contact with something rather wider, that is, the responsibility of those who have knowledge towards those who, for various reasons, do not. An interesting example of this kind of responsibility arose when knowledge of the Greek language first became widespread in Europe. There was great controversy concerning the translation of the Greek metanoia. The Vulgate had translated this as 'doing penance' and 'doing penance' had become an important part of Church life. This included the selling of indulgences. Tyndale's insistence on making known the mis-translation led to his imprisonment and death. He insisted that there could be no office of penance because repenting was something that only the individual could accomplish personally. Others, whose Greek was as good if not better than Tyndale's, remained silent, but not through fear (the fury of the protestant revolution had yet to come). Providing that 'doing penance' remained a sacrament of the Church (something that Tyndale denied), the Church had control over individual members. The Church's opposition to relinquishing this was all the more vehement because it was also especially lucrative. Tyndale felt that he had to speak out and declare that the Church was deliberately misleading people, by remaining silent concerning this mis-translation, and was doing so in order to have more control over its members.

Traditionally, power has resided in the Church and in the state, hence the perpetual fear of indoctrination by the Church and in politics. The Christian Church no longer has a power-base and the power of the state remains much as it was. However, are there other power bases, other organizations which have the ability to influence and control the lives of individuals in a way once practised by the Church?

In many respects, the methods of science are diametrically opposed to those practised by the indoc-trinator. The former belong to an open system of reasoning, the latter to a closed system. The very notion of 'scientific method', the process of 'conjecture and refutation', seems to guarantee that scientific knowledge could never ossify into a system of incontrovertible doctrines. Even the Russians had ultimately to abandon the genetic theories of Lysenko. Any attempt to cover up evidence in favour of a theory

153

would almost inevitably be doomed to failure because someone would sooner or later discover the attempts at deception.

Science no longer consists of dedicated, individual scientists devoting themselves to discovering what they believe to be 'truths' about the universe. Outwardly, scientific method remains the same, despite a greater reliance on instruments of great technological complexity, but science and the pursuit of scientific knowledge have become very expensive enterprises. The community of scientists with an open-minded desire for knowledge has become a scientific community with a power structure, seeking greater economic power by its relationship with the state. Scientists can pursue knowledge only if they are given the means of doing so.

This does not mean that scientists who are given means of support are going to do worse science or indulge in the falsification of results. It does mean, however, that scientists who hold views and theories which are contrary to those held by the scientific elite do not stand a chance of pursuing their enquiries. In the absence of total proof in science, it is the scientific community, the elite of the scientific establishment, who decide what will count as being true or worth pursuing.

However, much science today is not concerned with the 'pursuit of knowledge' or with 'knowledge for its own sake'. Indeed, it is doubtful if many scientists would hold the latter to be an ideal at all. Even if scientists believe in the intrinsic worth of knowledge, it is a socailly dangerous doctrine to hold. Increasingly, science is concerned with practical ends, in other words, with technology.

Technology is, of course, concerned with manipulation of nature and with the production of machines which enable people to have greater power over their surroundings and environment. If 'pure science' once followed ideals such as the 'pursuit of knowledge', technology has always been centred on people and devoted to the improvement of their lot on this earth. No doubt the industrial revolution shattered some of the Baconian ideals (of both Roger and Francis) of what technology could do to improve people's existence. However, the fact that technology is socially based, and is concerned with the manipulation or possible manipulation of the environment for the benefit of people, must bring technology into politics. Questions arise: who benefits, and at what cost?

Much controversy has arisen over the use of nuclear power and within this subject area are processes that we might recognize as indoctrination. For example, does the 'expert' representing the government deliberately withhold facts, 'massage the figures', deliberately misapply knowledge, in order to get people to agree to the plans that the government wishes to enforce? Does the average citizen feel powerless before the superior knowledge of the experts? Pressure groups have evolved in order to counter such feelings of mistrust towards the government and its 'experts'.

In particular areas, principally those of science and technology, the possibility of indoctrination increases. The development of specialized knowledge makes it difficult for the average person to challenge the evidence. In some cases, the ingredients for indoctrination are increased because particular groups of people may feel, or be persuaded, that they are working for the 'good' of others. Despite strict adherence by the medical profession to the ethical code implicit in the Hippocratic Oath, there are other ethical issues upon which this particular oath is silent. The general philosophy is that the doctor, and only the doctor, knows what is best for the patient. Here we have two potential ingredients of indoctrination: superior knowledge, and a lack of personal equality in the doctor-patient relationship because of the greater knowledge of the doctor.

This particular philosophy, inherent in the medical professions, becomes more dangerous when allied to government policy and to the wealth and power of drug companies. A whooping cough vaccine was introduced with the entirely laudable hope that it would eventually eradicate whooping cough and prevent death amongst small children. Unfortunately, some children suffered brain damage as a side-effect of the immunization programme. Because of the general good which would come from such a programme, i.e. that children on the whole would benefit and the overall death-rate from whooping cough be reduced, there was a deliberate 'conspiracy of silence' regarding the possible adverse effects in some children. In other words, it was decided by the medical advisers to the Department of Health that some children were 'expendable' for the general good.

We are, of course, correct in our decision to be wary of indoctrination but our preoccupation with politics and religion, as the areas where this is most likely to occur, is outmoded. Indoctrination can occur wherever there is a power structure which feels that it has an interest or profit (frequently both) in persuading people to accept a particular belief as being 'indubitably true'. The situation is made worse by the form that this indoctrination is likely to take, i.e. it may need fairly expert knowledge in any of the sciences. In practical terms, the teaching of politics is no more likely to lead to indoctrination than is the teaching of health education or economics.

Chapter nine

CONCLUSION

There has always been a tension between freedom and authority in political thought. Indeed, many liberal writers have thought of freedom as keeping authority at bay. The minimum state is thought of as the good state. On the other hand, numerous writers have attempted some sort of reconciliation between the two concepts. At the extreme, we find Hegel's argument that people achieve their greatest freedom by serving the state.

The first stance conjures up a picture of an idyllic, near anarchistic state where people co-operate and the state has the minimum function of maintaining security. This is a vision that John Locke sometimes reveals. The other stance is of a human beehive, where the human bees achieve fulfilment by serving the community and where all of their culture and aspirations are expressed through the structure of the state organization. In reality, of course, if we had a minimum state that was solely concerned with security, we would probably lay the ground for uncontrolled capitalism; if we followed Hegelianism, we would develop twentieth-century totalitarianism. In other words, the opposing nightmares arising from the dreams of Locke and Hegel are early capitalism and the totalitarianism of Stalin's USSR.

The concept of negative freedom, the idea of being left alone to get on with our life, has been extremely important in liberal thought. However, the problem with taking this idea too far is that it tends to isolate individuals from the public domain, so that they begin to look at politics as something separate from themselves and as something that other people can do. It leads them to look at politics as a murky area, concerned with compromise and deceit, and at the law as some unfortunate necessity to keep the few bad people at bay.

Conclusion

In many ways, the political approach is a more practical vision. It recognizes that there will be opposing interests in the community and that, if force is going to be avoided, there will be a need for bargaining, compromise, and conciliation. Political freedom lies not in avoiding contact with the necessity to participate in this process but in being given the opportunity to participate in such an activity. It is not a negative freedom from government but a positive freedom to govern. Political freedom is therefore the possibility of engaging in the activity of government but is also part of a special relationship between people.

It is a relationship that has grown up over the years in which people respect each other and generally trust each other. The rule of law, the institutional structure, the process of government, and the many debates and arguments are the formal expressions that work because they are part of a tradition and a traditional way of going about things. In a sense, the formal structure of the body politic can be understood only by working within it and by experiencing it. Freedom is not an anarchistic concept. It can exist only within a state of order and within a particular context. If, as we have argued, politics is the reconciliation of opposing interests, which are generally aiming at the public good, it can only exist under a combination of three conditions: order provided by government, within a tradition that allows opposing viewpoints and the possibility of dissent. Furthermore, the argument, dissent, and reconciliation must take place in public and not behind closed doors. It ought not be the prerogative of the few.[1]

We have argued that this freedom should be exercised by citizens. The word 'exercised' is important because it assumes that, as citizens, free people will wish to exercise their citizenship. They would possess 'arete' in the Greek sense of political virtue and would be prepared to move freely from the private to the public, with a concern for the public interest. Citizens have certain rights but also certain duties, and ideally will express their citizenship actively by showing civic virtue. We have argued that this virtue consists of being aware of the public debate and of being prepared to express opinions, or at least to give support to opinions, when a vital concern of the body politic is to be considered.

Thus the concept of being politically free is bound up with the notion of being active. Political freedom is simply the freedom to take part in debate and argument; the politically free society is a society that provides the framework for such controversy to take place. Politics in a sense is freedom; as Bernard Crick states, 'Politics are the public actions of free men.'[2]

Our analysis of the political community has contained a slight ambivalence. We have written of our having an obligation to a system that provides the condition for our form of life. We have also argued that a political system is really the public face of the ethical form of life and that when we feel that it has been achieved we tend to stop, rest, and be content. In stronger terms, to have a political obligation tends to make us apathetic: we accept that the system is all right and believe that the government can be left alone to get on with the activity of governing. It can be argued that this is because of our long tradition of having a political system, that in many other countries politics is a tender plant, which needs protection and eternal vigilance. The threat to politics in this country probably does not come from external aggression or from potential revolutions from the right or the left but from our desire for the quiet life and our resultant failure to exercise the duties of our citizenship. Government becomes used to making decisions without much argument; the bureaucracy enjoys developing rules and regulations without much opposition. Like ourselves, government ministers and bureaucrats enjoy the quiet life. However, in failing to carry out our duties, we are putting our rights at risk.

If the law is to continue to exist, it must be continually willed into existence. Obstructions to and infractions of the law must be prevented. We must not only will the law into existence but also actively protect it. The same applies to all of our political institutions. Unless they are used and their power is exercised and defended, they will become, like the Norman castles, historical memories whose significance degenerates into crumbling ruin. They will be the shell but not the living contents of the institution.

Our analysis has also highlighted another feature of politics. Politics does not separate a person's private life from the public, since, as we have argued, politics is an extension of one's social activity into the domain of public concern. To quote again from Bernard Crick,

> Politics is the public action of free men; free men are those who do, not merely can, live both publicly and privately. Men who have lost the capacity for public

action, who fear it or despise it, are not free, they are simply isolated and ineffectual.[3]

We have argued that politics is the public face of ethical individuals. The essence of ethical people is that they strive to be responsible for their own life, and to make their own decisions, while respecting the freedom and integrity of others. They are self-critical, creative, and active. In the public sphere, they respect order but are actively concerned with the public good. A political community is a community that enables such individuals to work together for such a good. If politics and the free society are to exist, there must be people who have political virtue and who are prepared to become involved and to speak out. Politics is as much threatened by individuals who keep quiet out of cowardice, laziness, or inexcusable ignorance as freedoms are eroded by a possible tyrant.

Education for citizenship is not an inappropriate option for the school curriculum or something that we should fear. If the vast majority of people are not to be treated as part of the masses and regulated and pushed in the directions that officials require, citizens must be shown how to act as citizens. If we value freedom, the political way of going about things, we must be prepared to preserve it. The preservation of freedom depends not only on educating our children, so that they may see its benefits and values, but also on developing in them a desire to work the institutions that maintain its existence.

NOTES AND REFERENCES

INTRODUCTION

1 Experience and Participation: Report of the Review Group of the Youth Service in England, Command 8686, London: Her Majesty's Stationery Office, 1982.
2 Political Education for Adults, Leicester, Advisory Council for Adult and Continuing Education, 1985.
3 The WEA and Political Education, London: Workers' Education Association, Jan. 1985.
4 Porter, A (ed.) (1983) Teaching Political Literacy: Implications for Teacher Training, Bedford Papers 16, London: Curriculum Review Unit.

1 POLITICAL EDUCATION: THE DEBATE

1 Peters, R.S. (1966) Ethics and Education, London: George Allen & Unwin.
  Peters sees education as inculcating states of mind desirable in themselves.
2 See Brownhill, R.J. (1983) Education and the Nature of Knowledge, London: Croom Helm, Ch.2.
3 Cited in Adamson, J.W. (1965) English Education 1789 to 1902, Cambridge: Cambridge University Press, p.317.
4 See Rich, E.E. (1970) The Education Act, 1870, London: Longman, p.79.
5 Oakeshott, M. (1933) Experience and Its Modes, Cambridge: Cambridge University Press.
  Hirst, P. (1974) Knowledge and the Curriculum, London: Routledge and Kegan Paul.
  Oakeshott develops the concept of modes of experience; Hirst develops it further with his concept of the forms of knowledge.
6 Haines, N. (1967) Person to Person, London: Macmillan.
7 There is an element of tacit, if not explicit, anti-democratic flavour amongst some of the people who advocated central planning and corporatism in the 1930s and 1940s. It was allied to the notion that a scientific approach to planning and social control was the panacea, and that decisions should be left to the experts.

See, for instance, Huxley, J. (1943) TVA, Adventure in Planning, London: Architectural Press (TVA: Tennessee Valley Authority)
and a discussion of this stance in Dival, C.M. (1985) 'Capitalising on "Science": Philosophical Ambiguity in Julian Huxley's Politics 1920-1950'. Unpublished Ph.D. thesis, Manchester University.

8   For instance, Heater, D. (1969) The Teaching of Politics, London: Methuen.

9   Brennan, T. (1981) Political Education and Democracy, Cambridge: Cambridge University Press. Brennan refers to a number of these arguments.

10   Stradling, R. (1977) The Political Awareness of the School Leaver, London: Hansard Society.

11   Paragraph 25 of address by Robert Dunn, M.P., Under-Secretary of State, Department of Education and Science at Politics Association Annual Conference, 14-16 September, 1984. Reprinted 1985 London: Politics Association.

12   Experience and Participation: Report of the Review Group on the Youth Service in England, Command 8686, London: Her Majesty's Stationery Office, 1982.

13   Ridley, F. (1985) 'What Adults? What Politics?', in Political Education for Adults, Leicester: Advisory Council for Adult and Continuing Education, p.13.

14   Oakeshott, M. (1962) 'Political Education', in Rationalism in Politics and Other Essays, London: Methuen, pp. 111-36.

15   Porter, A. (ed.) (1983) Teaching Political Literacy: Implications for Teacher Training, Bedford Papers 16, London: Curriculum Review Unit.

16   Beer, S. (1983) Modern British Politics, London: Faber & Faber.

17   See Dival, op. cit. (Note 7).

18   Scruton, R., Ellis-Jones, A., and O'Keefe, D. (1985) Education and Indoctrination, Harrow, Middlesex: Education Research Centre.

19   An argument used by Oakeshott in Experience and Its Modes, op. cit.

20   A claim made by Popper, K.R. (1961) in The Poverty of Historicism, London: Routledge & Kegan Paul.

21   See Popper, K.R. (1962) The Open Society and Its Enemies, London: Routledge & Kegan Paul.
For a critique by Popper on Marx, see Cornforth, N. (1977) The Open Philosophy and the Open Society,

London: Lawrence & Wishart.

22 Hayek, F. (1976) <u>Law, Legislation and Liberty</u>, London: Routledge & Kegan Paul, Vol.2.
Chapter 9 argues that the concept of social justice is vacuous.

23 Feyerabend, P. (1975) <u>Beyond Method</u>, London: New Left Books.
See also Kuhn, T.S. (1970) <u>The Structure of Scientific Revolutions</u>, Chicago: Chicago University Press
and Polanyi, M. (1958) <u>Personal Knowledge</u>, London: Routledge & Kegan Paul.

24 Hirst, op. cit.

25 Brownhill, R.J. (1973) 'Political Education in Michael Polanyi's Theory of Education', <u>Educational Theory</u> Vol. 24, No. 4, Fall, pp.303-9.

26 A discussion of Oakeshott's and Polanyi's ideas appears in Brownhill's <u>Education and the Nature of Knowledge</u>, op. cit.
See also Peters, R.S. (1968) 'Michael Oakeshott's Philosophy of Education', in P. King and B.C. Parekh (eds) <u>Politics and Experience</u>, Cambridge: Cambridge University Press, pp. 43-63.

27 An idea akin to Aristotle's notion about developing the ability to undertake moral actions.

28 Entwistle, H. (1971) <u>Political Education in a Democracy</u>, London: Routledge & Kegan Paul.
Entwistle also recognizes this danger.

29 Polanyi, M. (1981) <u>The Logic of Liberty</u>, London: Routledge & Kegan Paul, p.30

30 Ibid., pp. 29,30.

31 Hence Mill's use of his 'infallibility argument'. As he believes that political communities are concerned with grasping the truth, the suppression of a truth claim must be because we think that the view is wrong and our own is true. The argument would be powerful in a community that claimed a true doctrine but in a community that is not concerned with grasping the truth suppression of a view could be for security reasons, or bloody-mindedness, and might have no connection with the truth or with a claim of infallibility.

32 See Brownhill, R.J. (1977) 'Freedom and Authority: The Political Philosophy of Michael Polanyi', <u>The Journal of the British Society for Phenomenology</u> Vol. 8, No. 3, Oct., pp. 153-63.

163

2 THE MORAL BASE OF POLITICS AND POLITICAL EDUCATION

1 Feyerabend, P. (1975) Beyond Method, London: New Left Books.
2 See O'Hear, A. (1985) Wha⁺ is Philosophy? London: Pelican.
and Brown, A. (1986) Modern Political Philosophy, London: Penguin.
3 Rawls, J. (1972) A Theory of Justice, Oxford: Oxford University Press.
4 See Mill, J.S. 'On Liberty' in Utilitarianism, Liberty and Representative Government, London: Everyman, Dent, 1910, p.69.
5 D'Entrèves, A.P. (1968) 'On the Nature of Political Obligation', Philosophy, XLIII: 309-23.
6 Bentham, J. (1948) Fragment on Government, (W. Harrison ed.), Oxford: Oxford University Press, p.107.
7 Rousseau, J.J. (1973) 'The Social Contract', Book I, Ch.III, in The Social Contract and Discourses (G.D.H. Cole tr.), London: Dent.
8 Bentham, op. cit., Ch.I, Sect.1.
9 Ross, A. (1959) On Law and Justice, Berkeley: University of California, pp. 53-5.
10 Hart, H.L.A. (1961) uses this idea in The Concept of Law, Oxford: Clarendon Press.
11 Lucas, J.R. (1966) The Principles of Politics, Oxford: Clarendon Press.
Lucas points out that if a government is legitimate and on the whole acts in accordance with the shared values of the community, we will give it the benefit of the doubt when it undertakes questionable action. If it is illegal and not following shared values, we should never give it the benefit of the doubt and should be continually critical of its actions.
12 Polanyi, M. (1951) The Logic of Liberty, London: Routledge & Kegan Paul, p.30.
He believes that in an ideal community the institutions and laws will reflect public morality.
13 Taylor, P.W. (1961) Normative Discourse, Englewood Cliffs, New Jersey: Prentice-Hall.
Taylor uses the term 'way of life' in the same way as we have used the term 'form of life'.
14 Devlin, P. (1959) The Enforcement of Morals, Proceedings of the British Academy, Oxford: Oxford University

Press.
He would argue, however, that behaviour that is thought to be immoral and therefore opposed to the 'public conscience' could be considered to be against the public interest.

15   Griffith, J.A.C. (1977) The Politics of the Judiciary, Glasgow: Collins Fontana.
16   A view contrary to that of the legal positivists.
17   Goodhart, A.L. (1953) English Law and the Moral Law, London: Stevens & Sons.
Goodhart argues that the obligations to the law lie in its moral foundation.

3   TEACHING, LEARNING, AND LIBERAL EDUCATION

1   The examples are taken from Brennan, J. (1977) The Open Texture of Moral Concepts, London: Macmillan.
2   Oakeshott, M. (1933) Experience and its Modes, Cambridge: Cambridge University Press.
3   Hirst, P. (1974) Knowledge and the Curriculum, London: Routledge & Kegan Paul.
O'Hear, A. (1981) Education, Society and Nature, London: Routledge & Kegan Paul.
Hirst develops a similar argument to Oakeshott but calls the modes 'forms of knowledge'. O'Hear argues convincingly that these forms are really 'public forms of experience'.
4   In particular, Polanyi, M. (1958) Personal Knowledge, London: Routledge & Kegan Paul.
5   Marx, K. (1958) 'The Eighteenth Brumaire of Louis Bonaparte', in K. Marx and F. Engels, Selected Works, Vol. 1, London: Lawrence & Wishart.
6   Polanyi, M. (1959) The Study of Man, London: Routledge & Kegan Paul.
Polanyi argues that all judgements take place within an interpretative framework.
7   Polanyi, Personal Knowledge, op. cit., p.103.
8   Polanyi believes that he is revealing the logical structure of tacit knowing by his from-to analysis but it really is an explanation of how we develop an understanding of tacit integration.
See Harré, R. (1977) 'The Structure of Tacit Knowledge', Journal of the British Society for Phenomenology, Vol.8, No. 3, pp.172-7.

9   An expression used by Poteat, W.H. (1985) <u>Polanyian Meditations: In Search of a Post-Critical Logic,</u> Durham, North Carolina: Duke University Press.
10 Oakeshott, M. (1967) 'Learning and Teaching', in R.S. Peters (ed.) <u>The Concept of Education</u>, London: Routledge & Kegan Paul.
11 Polanyi, M. (1962) 'The Republic of Science', <u>Minerva</u> Vol. 1, Oct.
12 See a development of this argument in Brownhill, R. (1983) <u>Education and the Nature of Knowledge</u>, London: Croom Helm, Ch.4.
13 See Brownhill, R. (1977) 'Freedom and Authority: The Political Philosophy of Michael Polanyi', <u>Journal of the British Society for Phenomenology</u> Vol. 8, No.3, Oct.

4   THE POLITICAL COMMUNITY

1   Crick, B. (1964) <u>In Defence of Politics</u>, London: Pelican, p.18
2   Mill, J.S. (1910) 'On Liberty' in <u>Utilitarianism, Liberty and Representative Government</u>, London: Everyman, Dent, p.69.
3   Aristotle, <u>Politics</u>, Book III (J. Warrington ed./tr.), London: Everyman, Dent 1959, p.73.
4   Ibid., note 1, p. 88.
5   Crick, op.cit., p.18.
6   Nelson, W.N. (1974) 'Special Rights, General Rights, and Social Justice', <u>Philosophy and Public Affairs</u> Vol. 3, No. 4, Summer.
7   See Singer, P. (1979) <u>Practical Ethics</u>, Cambridge: Cambridge University Press.
8   Lucas, J.R. (1966) <u>The Principles of Politics</u>, Oxford: Clarendon Press.
9   Hart, H.L.A. (1961) <u>The Concept of Law</u>, Oxford: Clarendon Press.
10 Popper, K.R. (1959) <u>The Logic of Scientific Discovery</u>, New York: Basic Books.
11 Rawls, J. (1972) <u>A Theory of Justice</u>, Oxford: Oxford University Press.
12 An argument developed in much greater detail by Wyllie, W.E. (1983) 'An Enquiry into the Relationship between the Authority of the State and the Freedom of the Individual', Unpublished Ph.D. thesis, Surrey University.

13 See Mabbott, J.D. (1967) The State and the Citizen, London: Hutchinson.

14 See Gough, J.W. (1957) The Social Contract, Oxford: Oxford University Press.

15 Locke, J. The Second Treatise of Government (J.W. Gough, ed.), Oxford: Blackwell, 1956, Ch.XIII, para. 149.

16 See Murphy, J.G. (1970) Kant: The Philosophy of Right, London: Macmillan.

17 See Wyllie, op. cit., Ch. 8.

18 See McCloskey, H.J. (1968) 'Some Arguments for a Liberal Society', Philosophy Vol. XLIII, No. 163, pp. 324-44.
We shall give one example. Mill argues that liberty has extrinsic value: it is good because it leads to the attainment of other goods. Presumably this is a claim that can be empirically tested. Mill argues that it leads to progress and a lively belief. For the argument to be entirely successful, Mill must show that freedom is necessary for their attainment, that is, without freedom they cannot be attained. Consider that the USSR, without much political freedom, has made substantial advances in space research and technology. Elsewhere, many people have been led to religious fanaticism without having much freedom in choosing their religious beliefs. The weakness of Mill's argument is that it is of the form 'I like A because it leads to X'. It is a utilitarian argument which, if it can be shown that A does not always lead to X or that B sometimes leads to X, is reduced to 'I like whatever leads to X'. If A leads to X then A but if B leads to X then B: it is not a very good argument for always having A.

19 Polanyi, M. (1951) The Logic of Liberty, London: Routledge & Kegan Paul.

20 Polanyi, M. (1958) Personal Knowledge, London: Routledge & Kegan Paul.
Huxley, J. (1957) Religion without Revelation, London: Max Parish.
Huxley, with his theory of evolutionary ethics, argues about people's moral improvement.
Hardy, A. (1984) Darwin and the Spirit of Man, London: Collins.
Hardy uses Polanyi's arguments to explain the spiritual development of people.

Marx is really arguing in a similar way, although he is

looking at the evolution of society rather than people. The free society is the end of the process of historical evolution whereas capitalist society prevents people from being free.

5   THE NATURE OF POLITICAL ARGUMENT

1   Hume, D. Treatise on Human Nature (L.A. Selby Bigge, ed.), Oxford: Clarendon Press, 1906.
2   Popper, K.R. (1959), The Logic of Scientific Discovery, New York: Basic Books.
3   Hume, op. cit. See also Huson, W.D. (ed.) (1969) The Is/Ought Question, London: Macmillan.
4   Aristotle, The Rhetorica (R. Roberts tr.), Oxford: Oxford University Press, 1924, Book 1, passim.
5   Hume, op.cit.
6   Oakeshott, M. (1965) 'Rationalism in Politics: A Reply to Professor Raphael', Political Studies 13: 89-92
7   See Lucas, J.R. (1966) The Principles of Politics, Oxford: Clarendon Press for a development of this argument.
8   See Haines, N. (1969) 'Situational Method: A Proposal for Political Education in Democracy', Educational Theory, Vol. 19, Winter, No. 1,
     and Brownhill, R.J. (1971) 'Situational Method: An Experiment', Educational Theory, Vol. 21, Summer No. 3.
     Also Haines, N. (1967) Person to Person, London: Macmillan.
9   Taylor, P.W. (1961) Normative Discourse, Englewood Cliffs, New Jersey: Prentice-Hall.

6   THE POLITICAL CURRICULUM

1   Porter, A. (ed.) (1983) Teaching Political Literacy: Implications for Teacher Training, Bedford Papers 16, London: Curriculum Review Units.
2   Stradling, R. (1976) 'Political Education in the 11 to 16 Curriculum', Cambridge Journal of Education, Vol. 8, No. 283, Michaelmas term, p. 106.
3   De Jouvenel, B. (1963) The Pure Theory of Politics, Cambridge: Cambridge University Press, p.187.
4   Ibid., p. 140.

5   Hart, H.L.A. (1961) The Concept of Law, Oxford: Clarendon Press.
6   Singer, P. (1979) Practical Ethics, Cambridge: Cambridge University Press.
7   A number of writers make a similar distinction.
    See Rousseau, J.J. 'The Social Contract', Book II, Ch. VI, in The Social Contract and Discourses (G.D.H. Cole tr.), London: Dent, 1973, where a distinction is made between an act of sovereignty (universal) and an act of magistracy (particular).
    Also Hayek, F.A. (1968) 'The Confusion of Language in Political Thought', Occasional Paper 20, London: Institute of Economic Affairs, p.15, where a distinction is made between nomos, a universal rule of conduct, and thesis, which is any rule that relates to particular people or is in the service of the end of rulers.
8   See Hill, M. (1976) The State, Administration and the Individual, London: Fontana, for an examination of this whole area.
9   Lenin, V.I. (n.d.) What is to be done? Moscow: Foreign Languages Publishing House.

7   IMPARTIALITY, BIAS, AND CONTROVERSIAL ISSUES

1   Proudhon, P.J. (1974) 'De la Justice', in J. Muglioni (ed.) Justice et Liberté, Vendôme: Presses Universitaires de France.
2   Aristotle, 'Nicomachean Ethics', in W.D. Ross and J.A. Smith (eds) The Works of Aristotle, Vol. IX, Oxford: Oxford University Press, 1925.
3   Mill, J.S. 'On Liberty' in Utilitarianism, Liberty and Representative Government, London: Everyman, Dent, 1910.
4   Ruddock, J. (1983) The Humanities Curriculum Project: An Introduction, London: Schools Council Publications.
5   Robert Stradling points out that an over-powerful advocacy of a particular line may turn off the listener and thereby be counter-productive.
    See Stradling, R. (1984) Teaching Controversial Issues, London: Edward Arnold, p.65.
6   Wellington, J. (1985) 'Including the nuclear issue in the curriculum: a balanced approach', Cambridge Journal of Education, Vol. 15, No. 3, pp. 127-33
7   David Hume would also argue that we would be

irrational if we failed to follow the necessary means to bring about the desired end.

8   INDOCTRINATION

1   The Newcastle Report, London: Eyre & Spottiswood, 1861, p. 300.
2   Russell, B.(1932) Education and the Social Order, London: George Allen & Unwin, Ch. XV.
3   Hare, R.M. (1964) 'Adolescents into Adults', in T.B. Hollins (ed.) The Aims of Education, Manchester: Manchester University Press.
4   Wilson, J. (1964) 'Education and Indoctrination', in Hollins, op.cit.
5   Peters, R.S. (1966) Ethics and Education, London: George Allen & Unwin.
6   Ayer, A.J. (1936) Language, Truth and Logic, London: Victor Gollancz.
7   Popper, K.R. (1963) Conjectures and Refutations, London: Routledge & Kegan Paul.
8   Peirce, C.S. (1957) Essays in the Philosophy of Science, New York: Bobbs-Merrill
9   Buber, M. (1947) Between Man and Man, London: Collins.

9   CONCLUSION

1   A system could be classed as democratic but not necessarily political; it could also, to some degree, be political without being democratic.
2   Crick, B. (1964) In Defence of Politics, London: Pelican, p.18.
3   Ibid.

INDEX

achievement 54, 57, 123, 124, 132, 139
aims: education 23, 25, 29, 31; science 25
apathy 3, 9, 40
apprenticeship 16, 17, 51
argument: deductive 79-87 passim, 96; inductive 80, 82; normative 41-4, 98-102; political 69, 76, 79-100; political education 1-22: against 11-21, in favour 4-10, 21-2; rational 41-4, 106, 110; scientific 80-7 passim; teaching political 97-9
Aristotle 10, 11, 28, 29, 61, 62, 82-4 passim, 88, 90, 91, 100
authority 59, 60, 69-72 passim, 157
autonomy 70, 123, 124, 129, 130
Ayer, A.J. 170

Bacon, F. 154
Bacon, R. 154
Beer, S. 11, 162
beliefs: irrational 41, 137-8; rational 41, 137-8; reasonable 99, 135-7; unreasonable 135-7
Bentham, J. 32, 33, 46, 164
bias 135-42
Brennan, J. 32, 33, 46, 164
Brennan, T. 162
Brown, A. 164
Brownhill, R.J. vii, 161, 163, 166, 168
Buber, M. 152, 170

Burke, E. 17, 95, 137

Campaign for Nuclear Disarmament 118, 119
central planning 161
chartism 2
citizenship vii, 8, 21, 30, 31, 34, 59, 61, 62, 69-76
civic virtue 62
closed associations 31
Cole, G.D.H. 164, 169
collectivism 5, 9
commitment 14, 15, 19, 21, 32, 51, 127, 130
community: intellectual 17-21, 54-6 passim; moral 22; political vii, 5, 11, 16, 17, 19-22, 34, 58-78, 110, 167: justification 76-8, 167, model 66-8, Marxist model 75-6, valuing 19, 20, 31-41, 70, 110
compromise 36, 98
contract 64-5
controversial issues 132-3
Copernican revolution 82
Cornforth, N. 162
corporatism 161
councillors 117-18
Crick, B. 7, 56, 60, 62, 68, 77, 78, 103, 159, 160, 170
criticism 16, 18
Crito 64
curriculum: hidden 1, 3; political viii, 58, 103-22: ethical base 110, 111-15

decision procedure 34, 56,